PRESENTED TO

FROM

DATE

Cooking Up
A Classic Christmas
Santa's Secrets for an Unforgettable Holiday!

Library of Congress Catalog Number: 2006922064
ISBN: 978-0-87197-526-3

Art Director: Steve Newman
Book Design: Brad Whitfield and Susan Breining
Project Editor: Tanis Westbrook

Manufactured in China
First Printing: 2006
Second Printing: 2007

*Thank you to the food writers, cookbook authors, and individuals
who graciously submitted their stories and family memories
for inclusion in this cookbook. We regret that we were not able
to use all the recipes and stories we received.*

About the Artist

R. J. (Ralph) McDonald is one of our country's most highly respected wildlife artists. For more than thirty years, knowledgeable art collectors have enthusiastically collected his paintings, giclees, and limited edition prints. Among these collectors are a chief justice of the United States Supreme Court, two state governors, several senators and congressmen, as well as movie stars, corporations, and business leaders. Add to this group the tens of thousands of other collectors who appreciate and collect McDonald's realistic paintings and limited edition prints of North American wildlife.

McDonald received his formal art education at The Harris Art School. After graduating from Harris he stayed on with the school as an instructor for two years before entering the commercial art field. For several years he enjoyed a successful career as a commercial artist, but he did not enjoy having to paint only those subjects that his clients ordered. The artist in him yearned to create paintings of the subjects that interested him, the birds and animals of Tennessee. So he left the security of commercial art to become a wildlife artist. His career received a substantial boost when the governor of Tennessee commissioned him to paint the official portrait of the state's bird, the mockingbird.

Ralph has enjoyed a very successful career, but he has always felt an appreciation and debt to the birds and animals whose images have contributed so much to his success. Ducks Unlimited named him its National Artist of the Year in 1981. Over the years the sale of his paintings and prints by conservation organizations have raised over fifteen million dollars to help fund their projects. His "Green Wing" series is the most profitable print series in Ducks Unlimited's history. In appreciation for his contributions to wildlife, Ducks Unlimited and the Tennessee Wildlife Resources Agency named a major wildlife management area in Middle Tennessee in his honor.

McDonald's work has been featured at numerous major art shows and exhibitions throughout the country, among them are Game Conservation International, the Ducks Unlimited National Wildlife Art Show, Safari Club International and the Easton Waterfowl Festival. He has also been the featured artist of the year at the Southeastern Wildlife Exposition (1988), the World Wildlife Exposition (1991), the Southern Wildlife Exposition (1993), and the Ducks Unlimited Great Outdoors Festival (1998).

For the past twelve years Ralph has produced paintings of a young boy or girl in a waterfowl setting. Prints of these paintings have been auctioned at Ducks Unlimited's dinners and the sales of these prints have raised over fifteen million dollars for the organization's conservation projects.

In 2004, the Tennessee Alumni asked Ralph to produce a series of prints for their organization to sell to raise funds for four-year college scholarships for deserving students.

In 2006, McDonald was named Ducks Unlimited's International Artist of the Year.

Introduction

Community cookbooks have been around since the Civil War, offering cooks a way to share their favorite recipes and readers a glimpse into the life of a community.

Community cookbooks are dependable for their creative collections of tried-and-true recipes — readers often consume them like novels. FRP (Favorite Recipes Press) has been pleased to work with and support thousands of community cookbook publishers over the past four decades, helping them raise the funds that go to great causes across the nation.

In Cooking Up A Classic Christmas, we are proud to share with you the long-awaited, first compilation cookbook of favorite recipes from the publishers of some of our best and best-known cookbooks. This cookbook includes a collection of favorite recipes especially fitting for the holiday table, along with stories, traditions and memories of holidays past, fun holiday menus, and kitchen-savvy tips. The community cookbooks from which the recipes in this book are taken represent communities from all over the United States and are some of the best selling cookbooks of all time, ranging in age from forty-seven years old and over a million copies in print, to the brand new and just arriving on shelves.

It is our holiday wish that Cooking Up A Classic Christmas brings joy, delicious food, and wonderful traditions and memories to you and your family for many years to come!

Table of Contents

Hope for the Holidays

Ever wonder what kinds of lessons your holiday celebration teaches your children and whether all your effects are worth the effort? Here's the holiday lesson I remember most vividly. I call it The Year I was Really Bad.

I was nine. I don't know what came over me. I was really bad. I didn't listen to my mother. I willfully declined to follow directions. I got a very low grade in one of my classes. My room perpetually looked like a shipwreck. I didn't ask permission. I was mean to a gawky new kid at school. I ate during the table grace. I wouldn't shake the hands of grown-ups or look them in the eye and say "nice to meet you." I might as well have been fourteen.

My mother must have been exasperated. It was still just October when she began warning me about my stocking being filled with lumps of coal. Often during those next months, I was reminded of that coal and of other bad things that could be in a stocking — ashes and switches.

It must not have worked. Near Christmas, I did something really bad. I was not present at our agreed-upon pick-up location after an outing with friends. She had expected to drive right up and collect me up at the curb, but I wasn't there. She was frantic, and worse, she had my baby brother with her, who, at almost two years, was not walking. Collapsible strollers were a decade away, so she hauled that heavy baby all over the shopping mall looking for me, and when she found me, she was livid.

No two ways about it: Santa would definitely hear about this. I would get coal, ashes, and switches in my stocking. My sentence had been passed, and there was no court of appeal.

Christmas morning rolled around, and instead of jumping out of bed and charging downstairs, I was leisurely in waking my brothers and strolling down to the tree. There would be nothing for me. I had been naughty, not nice.

My stocking was hanging from the mantle, and as expected, it was indeed lumpy.
I didn't really know what coal was — our ancient, rambling, drafty house had pathetic
electric wall heaters, not a mighty basement furnace — but it didn't sound nice.
Mother had definitely used the word "lumps of coal." It was certainly lumpy,
and that might have been a switch poking out the top, whatever a switch was.

I walked grimly to the stocking, like a doomed prisoner. I would take this hard sentence
and try to be gracious about it, so as not to ruin the family's enjoyment of their gifts.

But wait — it wasn't a switch, maybe. It looked like, IT WAS, a candy cane! And when
I hefted the stocking, it wasn't light like ashes, it was heavy and it clonked, like nuts.
And there was a deck of cards, and a diary, and a four-color ink pen. My stocking
wasn't full of coal! Santa had pardoned me! I was going to have Christmas after all!
I felt like I had been freed.

My mother's gone now, so I can only wonder whether my parents fretted over
the ashes and switches and coal. Did they ponder teaching me a hard lesson
about proper behavior, or a lesson in grace and mercy? Did they think a stocking
full of gifts would spoil me, leading to a life of crime and an untimely end?

Besides the few details of Christmas, what I really remember is how lucky,
how very, very lucky I felt, and how wonderful the gift of Christmas spirit is.

May Cooking Up a Classic Christmas help fill your holidays with all the
gifts of Christmas —the warmth of family and food, the special blessings
of the season, and, above all, grace that is the Christmas spirit.

NICKI PENDLETON WOOD

Open House

As the seasons change, I find myself in our dining room continuing a family tradition: placing seasonal decorations on our dining room table. This was my parents' table, and it holds so many memories—sort of a mahogany "Ghost of Celebrations Past." When I was a little girl, the table was the herald of things to come. Usually, it sat quiet in our dining room with one or two leaves inserted. But every once in a while the table would almost come to life and tell me that good times were nearly here.

Best of all was when the table suddenly sprouted a long red runner, covered with hundreds of wooden German figurines, music boxes, and candles. It made no difference what the calendar or weatherman said: this was the sign that Christmas was coming. The table told of cookies to bake, candy to make, presents to wrap, and gifts to bake. For us, Christmas Day was very special, but the caroling party we held the week before Christmas is what I remember most of all.

We would invite relatives and friends for punch, wassail, and eggnog. A huge pot of rich beef stew would bubble on the stove while fresh bread baked in the oven; large salad bowls overflowed with greens dressed with garlic, oil, and vinegar—olfactory overload in the Gaiser family kitchen. When the carols were sung and our guests were about to depart, each child received a gingerbread man with his or her name on it—a special treat which was never known to last much beyond the doorstep.

Now, the caroling is done, and Mom, Dad, and most of their friends are gone to rest, but the table remains to tell of the good times we had. And I still set the table first. Before the tree can be trimmed or the lights lit, the runner must be placed down the center of the table and the figurines, candles, and bows carefully arranged. Only then can the recipes be re-created and the party begun. I do not know why, but that is the way it has to be. It is the Gaiser family way.

KRISTINA GAISER CONNER

Yuletide Open House

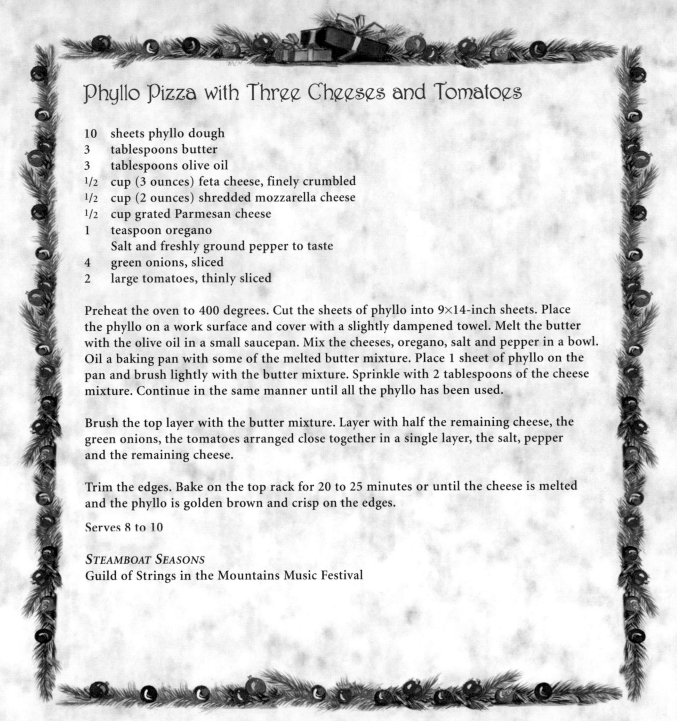

Phyllo Pizza with Three Cheeses and Tomatoes

10 sheets phyllo dough
3 tablespoons butter
3 tablespoons olive oil
1/2 cup (3 ounces) feta cheese, finely crumbled
1/2 cup (2 ounces) shredded mozzarella cheese
1/2 cup grated Parmesan cheese
1 teaspoon oregano
  Salt and freshly ground pepper to taste
4 green onions, sliced
2 large tomatoes, thinly sliced

Preheat the oven to 400 degrees. Cut the sheets of phyllo into 9×14-inch sheets. Place the phyllo on a work surface and cover with a slightly dampened towel. Melt the butter with the olive oil in a small saucepan. Mix the cheeses, oregano, salt and pepper in a bowl. Oil a baking pan with some of the melted butter mixture. Place 1 sheet of phyllo on the pan and brush lightly with the butter mixture. Sprinkle with 2 tablespoons of the cheese mixture. Continue in the same manner until all the phyllo has been used.

Brush the top layer with the butter mixture. Layer with half the remaining cheese, the green onions, the tomatoes arranged close together in a single layer, the salt, pepper and the remaining cheese.

Trim the edges. Bake on the top rack for 20 to 25 minutes or until the cheese is melted and the phyllo is golden brown and crisp on the edges.

Serves 8 to 10

STEAMBOAT SEASONS
Guild of Strings in the Mountains Music Festival

Crispy Fried Eggplant and Mozzarella Finger Sandwiches

4   Japanese eggplant
6   tablespoons olive oil, divided
     Salt to taste
     Freshly ground pepper to taste
3   garlic cloves
1/2 cup fresh basil
1/4 cup flat-leaf parsley
1/8 teaspoon red pepper flakes
16   ounces fresh mozzarella cheese, cut into twenty 1/4-inch slices
3   eggs, lightly beaten
1   cup (4 ounces) grated Parmesan cheese
     Vegetable oil for frying

Preheat the oven to 425 degrees. Cut each eggplant on the diagonal into ten 1/2-inch slices. Brush the eggplant with 3 tablespoons of the olive oil. Sprinkle with salt and pepper. Arrange on a baking sheet. Bake for 15 minutes or until golden brown.

Combine the garlic, basil, parsley, red pepper flakes and remaining 3 tablespoons olive oil in a food processor and process until blended. Spread the herb mixture on half the eggplant slices. Top each prepared eggplant slice with a slice of mozzarella cheese and the remaining eggplant slices.

Dip the eggplant sandwiches in the beaten egg. Roll in the Parmesan cheese. Heat 1/2 inch oil in a skillet. Cook the eggplant sandwiches in the hot oil for 2 minutes on each side or until brown; drain. Serve warm.

Makes 20 finger sandwiches

DINING DAKOTA STYLE
The Junior League of Sioux Falls

Herb Crescent Rolls

2   cups crushed crisp rice cereal
1   tablespoon caraway seeds
1   tablespoon sesame seeds
1   teaspoon seasoned salt, or to taste
10 canned refrigerator biscuits
6   tablespoons margarine, melted

Preheat the oven to 400 degrees. Line a baking sheet with heavy-duty foil and spray lightly with nonstick cooking spray. Combine the cereal, caraway seeds, sesame seeds and seasoned salt in a bowl and mix well. Cut each biscuit horizontally into halves.

Dip each biscuit half into the melted margarine and coat with the cereal mixture. Arrange the biscuit halves in a single layer on the prepared baking sheet. Bake for 8 to 11 minutes or until puffed and golden brown.

Makes 20

Provisions & Politics
James K. Polk Memorial Association

Mushroom Buttons

1   pound bacon, crisp-fried and
    crumbled, or sausage, browned
8   ounces cream cheese, softened
2   tablespoons minced green onions
    Mushroom caps

Preheat the oven to 375 degrees. Combine the bacon, cream cheese and green onions in a bowl and mix well. Spoon the mixture into the mushroom caps. Arrange on a baking sheet. Bake for 15 to 18 minutes or until the mushrooms are tender but firm.

Makes a variable amount

Southern On Occasion
The Junior League of Cobb-Marietta

Teriyaki Meatballs

MEATBALLS

3   pounds ground pork
2   (8-ounce) cans drained, finely chopped water chestnuts
1¹/₂ cups finely chopped green onions
1   tablespoon finely chopped fresh or crystallized ginger
2   tablespoons salt
3   tablespoons soy sauce
4   lightly beaten eggs
1¹/₂ cups bread crumbs
¹/₄ cup cornstarch
¹/₂ cup vegetable oil

PINEAPPLE SAUCE

1   (8-ounce) can chopped pineapple
2   cups unsweetened pineapple juice
1   cup cider vinegar
¹/₄ cup soy sauce
²/₃ cup sugar
1¹/₂ cups beef broth
2   tablespoons finely chopped fresh or crystallized ginger
¹/₃ cup cornstarch
²/₃ cup cold water

For the meatballs, combine the pork, water chestnuts, green onions, ginger, salt, soy sauce and eggs in a large bowl. Mix well with your hands. Add the bread crumbs and mix until just combined; chill the mixture. Shape into 3/4- to 1-inch balls. Roll the meatballs in cornstarch. Brown the meatballs on all sides in hot oil in a large skillet. Remove the meatballs and put in a roasting pan. To freeze, place the meatballs in a single layer on the roasting pan and put into freezer bags when frozen. Take out as needed. Preheat the oven to 350 degrees. Bake the meatballs for 15 to 20 minutes or until cooked through.

For the sauce, combine the pineapple, pineapple juice, vinegar, soy sauce, sugar, beef broth and ginger in a large saucepan and bring to a boil. Combine the cornstarch with the water and stir into the boiling mixture. Continue cooking and stirring until the sauce is thick and clear. The sauce will keep in the refrigerator for up to a week.

To serve, place the meatballs in a chafing dish with enough sauce to coat the meatballs. Serve with wooden picks.

Makes 150 meatballs

OF TIDE AND THYME
The Junior League of Annapolis

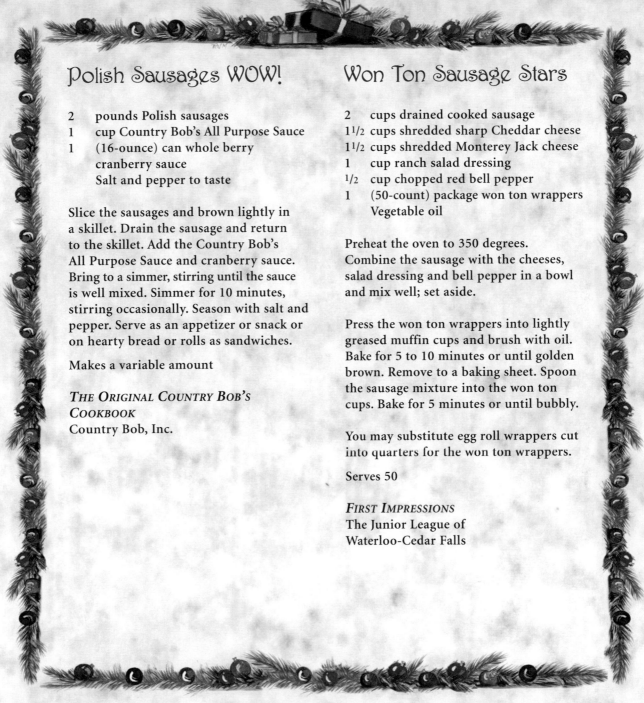

Polish Sausages WOW!

2   pounds Polish sausages
1   cup Country Bob's All Purpose Sauce
1   (16-ounce) can whole berry
     cranberry sauce
     Salt and pepper to taste

Slice the sausages and brown lightly in
a skillet. Drain the sausage and return
to the skillet. Add the Country Bob's
All Purpose Sauce and cranberry sauce.
Bring to a simmer, stirring until the sauce
is well mixed. Simmer for 10 minutes,
stirring occasionally. Season with salt and
pepper. Serve as an appetizer or snack or
on hearty bread or rolls as sandwiches.

Makes a variable amount

*THE ORIGINAL COUNTRY BOB'S
COOKBOOK*
Country Bob, Inc.

Won Ton Sausage Stars

2   cups drained cooked sausage
1½ cups shredded sharp Cheddar cheese
1½ cups shredded Monterey Jack cheese
1   cup ranch salad dressing
½   cup chopped red bell pepper
1   (50-count) package won ton wrappers
     Vegetable oil

Preheat the oven to 350 degrees.
Combine the sausage with the cheeses,
salad dressing and bell pepper in a bowl
and mix well; set aside.

Press the won ton wrappers into lightly
greased muffin cups and brush with oil.
Bake for 5 to 10 minutes or until golden
brown. Remove to a baking sheet. Spoon
the sausage mixture into the won ton
cups. Bake for 5 minutes or until bubbly.

You may substitute egg roll wrappers cut
into quarters for the won ton wrappers.

Serves 50

FIRST IMPRESSIONS
The Junior League of
Waterloo-Cedar Falls

Bite-Size Crab Quiches

1/2   pound crab meat, drained and
       flaked, or 2 (6-ounce) cans
       crab meat, drained and flaked
1   cup (4 ounces) shredded Swiss
       cheese or sharp Cheddar cheese
1/2   cup mayonnaise
2   tablespoons chopped green onions
1   tablespoon finely chopped red or
       green bell pepper
1   teaspoon fresh lemon juice
1/2   teaspoon curry powder
1   recipe Cream Cheese Crust

Combine the crab meat, cheese,
mayonnaise, green onions, bell pepper,
lemon juice and curry powder in a bowl
and mix well. Chill the mixture while
preparing the Cream Cheese Crust.
Preheat the oven to 400 degrees. Roll
the dough 1/8 inch thick on a floured
surface. Cut into 2-inch rounds. Press
each round on the bottom and up the
side of 36 miniature muffin cups. Spoon
the crab meat filling evenly into the
cups. Bake on the lowest oven rack for
15 minutes or until golden brown.
Serve hot.

Makes 36 servings

TASTES, TALES AND TRADITIONS
Palo Alto Auxiliary

Cream Cheese Crust

1/2   cup (1 stick) butter, chilled
3   ounces cream cheese, chilled
1   cup all-purpose flour

Combine the butter and cream cheese in
a food processor fitted with a steel blade
and process until smooth. Add the flour
and pulse just until blended. Shape the
dough into a smooth round on a sheet
of plastic wrap. Bring the plastic wrap
around the dough to wrap tightly. Chill
for 1 hour or until ready to bake. Let
stand at room temperature for a few
minutes before rolling.

Makes 36 tartlet shells or
1 (9-inch) piecrust

TASTES, TALES AND TRADITIONS
Palo Alto Auxiliary

Smoked Turkey Spread with Cranberries

8   ounces cream cheese, softened
1/4 cup mayonnaise
1   cup chopped smoked turkey
1   teaspoon minced green onion
1/2 cup chopped roasted pecans
1/4 cup chopped fresh parsley
1/4 cup dried cranberries
     Kosher salt and freshly ground
     pepper to taste

Combine the cream cheese and mayonnaise in a medium bowl and mix well. Add the turkey and green onion and mix well. Stir in the pecans, parsley, cranberries, kosher salt and pepper. Spoon the mixture into a small serving bowl. Chill, covered, until ready to serve. Garnish with parsley sprigs. Serve with table water crackers. May be prepared up to 1 day in advance.

Makes about 2 cups

GRAND TEMPTATIONS
The Junior League of Grand Rapids

Lobster Artichoke Dip

16   ounces cream cheese, softened
2   cups mayonnaise
12   ounces frozen canned lobster,
     thawed and drained
1   (14-ounce) can artichoke hearts,
     drained and chopped
1 1/2 cups (6 ounces) grated
     Parmesan cheese
2/3 cup chopped onion

Preheat the oven to 375 degrees. Blend the cream cheese and mayonnaise in a large bowl until smooth. Shred the lobster with your fingers, discarding any cartilage. Add the lobster, artichoke hearts, Parmesan cheese and onion to the mayonnaise mixture and mix well. Spoon into a 2-quart baking dish. Bake for 30 to 40 minutes or until bubbly and heated through. Serve with crackers and bagel chips.

Serves 14 to 16

ONCE UPON A TIME
The Junior League of Evansville

You may substitute 12 ounces imitation crab meat or canned crab meat, drained, for the frozen canned lobster.

Marinated Cheese Trio

CONFETTI MARINADE

1/2 cup olive oil
1/2 cup red wine vinegar
1/4 cup fresh lime juice
1   teaspoon sugar
1/2 teaspoon salt
1/2 teaspoon freshly ground pepper
1/2 cup drained and chopped roasted
     red bell peppers
3   green onions with stems, minced
3   tablespoons chopped parsley

CHEESE

1   (8-ounce) block sharp
     Cheddar cheese
1   (8-ounce) block Pepper Jack cheese
1   (8-ounce) package cream cheese
1/4 cup sliced kalamata olives

To prepare the marinade, combine the olive oil, vinegar and lime juice in a bowl and whisk until smooth. Whisk in the sugar, salt and pepper. Add the roasted peppers, green onions and parsley and mix well.

To prepare the cheese, cut the block of Cheddar cheese into halves lengthwise. Cut the halves crosswise into 1/4-inch slices. Repeat with the Pepper Jack cheese and cream cheese. Stand the cheese slices on edge to form a log in a shallow dish lined with plastic wrap, alternating the cheeses. Spoon the marinade over the top. Marinate, covered, in the refrigerator for 8 hours or longer.

Remove the log to a serving plate using the plastic wrap to hold the log together. Remove the plastic wrap. Spoon some of the marinade over the top. Sprinkle with the olives and serve with assorted crackers.

Serves 6 to 8

BEACH APPÉTIT
The Junior League of the Emerald Coast

Sun-Dried Tomato and Pesto Boursin Torta

BASIL PESTO
3   medium garlic cloves
2   tablespoons pine nuts
1   cup (1^1/$_2$ ounces) fresh basil leaves
^{1}/$_2$ cup (2 ounces) freshly grated
     Parmesan cheese
^{1}/$_3$ cup extra-virgin olive oil

TORTA AND ASSEMBLY
1   (8-ounce) jar sun-dried
     tomatoes, drained

24   ounces cream cheese, softened
6   tablespoons butter or
     margarine, softened
4   large garlic cloves, crushed
     and chopped
1   teaspoon each thyme, basil,
     oregano, dill weed, marjoram and
     salt-free seasoning mix
^{1}/$_3$ teaspoon freshly ground pepper
1   sprig of basil

For the pesto, add the garlic cloves 1 at a time to a food processor, processing constantly until finely chopped. Add the pine nuts, basil and cheese. Process until the basil is chopped. Add the olive oil gradually, processing constantly until blended and scraping the side of the bowl as needed. Spoon the pesto into a covered container. Store in the refrigerator for up to 2 days. Bring to room temperature before using.

For the torta, line a loaf pan with plastic wrap, allowing enough overhang to cover the torta. Pat the sun-dried tomatoes with paper towels and chop. Beat the cream cheese and butter in a mixing bowl until smooth, scraping the bowl occasionally. Add the garlic, thyme, basil, oregano, dill weed, marjoram, seasoning mix and pepper to the cream cheese mixture and beat until blended. Chill, covered, for 15 minutes. Spread half the cream cheese mixture in the prepared loaf pan. Spread with the pesto. Sprinkle with ^{1}/$_4$ cup of the sun-dried tomatoes. Layer with the remaining cream cheese mixture and smooth with a knife. Cover with the plastic wrap. Chill for 4 hours or longer. Invert the torta onto a serving platter, discarding the plastic wrap. Sprinkle with the remaining sun-dried tomatoes and top with the sprig of basil. Serve with assorted party crackers. You may substitute one 3- or 4-ounce jar of commercially prepared basil pesto for the homemade pesto. This may be prepared up to 3 days ahead, and it will keep for up to 7 days in the refrigerator.

Serves 12 to 15

PROVISIONS & POLITICS
James K. Polk Memorial Association

Baked Herb Havarti Cheese

2   tablespoons Dijon mustard
12   ounces Havarti cheese
1   tablespoon parsley flakes
1   tablespoon chopped fresh dill weed
1   teaspoon fennel seeds
1   teaspoon chopped fresh basil
1   sheet frozen puff pastry, thawed
1   egg, beaten

Spread the mustard over the cheese. Sprinkle with the parsley flakes, dill weed, fennel seeds and basil. Place the pastry over the top of the cheese and turn over. Wrap the cheese in the pastry to enclose as for a present, trimming excess pastry and brushing the seams with water to seal. Place seam side down on a plate. Chill, covered, in the refrigerator for 30 minutes or for up to 8 to 10 hours. Preheat the oven to 375 degrees. Place the pastry-wrapped cheese on a greased baking sheet. Bake for 20 minutes. Brush with the egg. Bake for 10 minutes. Remove from the oven and let stand for 5 minutes before serving. Serve with sliced pears and sliced Fuji or Golden Delicious apples. May also serve with assorted crackers.

Serves 12 to 15

SEABOARD TO SIDEBOARD
The Junior League of Wilmington

Savory Shrimp and Artichoke Dip

1   (14-ounce) can artichoke hearts, drained
6   ounces frozen precooked peeled small shrimp
3   ounces cream cheese, softened
1/2 cup mayonnaise
1/2 cup salsa
1/3 cup grated Parmesan cheese
1   red bell pepper, diced
     Green onion tops, thinly sliced

Preheat the oven to 350 degrees. Rinse and chop the artichoke hearts. Thaw the shrimp and squeeze dry in paper towels. Combine the artichoke hearts, shrimp, cream cheese, mayonnaise, salsa and Parmesan cheese in a large bowl and mix well. Spoon into a 9-inch pie plate or shallow baking dish. Bake for 20 minutes. Top with the bell pepper and green onions. Serve with tortilla chips or assorted fresh vegetables.

Serves 16

CELEBRATE COLORADO
Junior Service League of Grand Junction

Lib Wilhelm's Cheese Slaw

1   pound Swiss cheese,
    coarsely shredded
1   bunch green onions with
    tops, chopped
1/2 cup chopped mild banana peppers
1/2 cup finely chopped jalapeño peppers
    Mayonnaise
1   head cabbage

Combine the cheese, green onions, banana peppers and jalapeño peppers in a bowl. Add enough mayonnaise to bind and mix well. Store in the refrigerator for up to 1 week. Add additional mayonnaise if needed at serving time.

Hollow out the center of the cabbage and fold back the outer leaves. Spoon the cheese mixture into the center. Serve with corn chip scoops.

Serves 16

OH MY STARS!
The Junior League of Roanoke

Mississippi Sin

1   baguette French bread
1   (8-ounce) container French
    onion dip
2   cups (8 ounces) shredded sharp
    Cheddar cheese
8   ounces cream cheese, softened
1   (4-ounce) can chopped green
    chiles, drained

Preheat the oven to 350 degrees. Cut the top off the bread and reserve. Scoop out the bread from the center of the loaf; discard or reserve for use as bread crumbs. Mix the onion dip, Cheddar cheese, cream cheese and green chiles in a bowl. Spoon into the hollowed-out bread loaf and replace the top. Wrap in foil and place on a baking sheet. Bake for 1 hour. Remove the top of the bread. Serve with corn chips.

Serves 8

TAKE FIVE, A HOLIDAY COOKBOOK
Debbye Dabbs

Hot Pepper Peach Dip

2   (8-ounce) packages cream
     cheese, softened
1   (6-ounce) jar hot pepper peach jam
1   tablespoon chopped seeded
     jalapeño chile
1   teaspoon paprika
1   teaspoon chopped parsley
1   teaspoon dehydrated minced onion
2   cups (8 ounces) shredded
     mozzarella cheese

Blend the cream cheese, jam, jalapeño
chile, paprika, parsley and onion in a
large mixing bowl using a hand mixer
at medium speed. Spoon the dip into
2 serving bowls. Sprinkle half the
mozzarella cheese over each dip. Cover
the bowls and refrigerate until ready
to serve.

Serves 12

BEYOND THE RIM
The Junior League of Amarillo

Cranberry Salsa

1   (12-ounce) package fresh cranberries
1   jalapeño chile
     Grated zest of 1 orange
     (about 4 teaspoons)
     Grated zest of 1 lemon
     (about 1 teaspoon)
     Juice of 1/2 orange
     Juice of 1/2 lime
1/2 cup sugar
1/2 cup chopped red onion
     Dash of salt

Rinse the cranberries, discarding any
soft or bruised berries. Seed and chop the
jalapeño chile. Combine the cranberries,
jalapeño chile, orange zest, lemon zest,
orange juice, lime juice, sugar, onion and
salt in a food processor. Process until of
the desired consistency. Prepare this 1 to
2 days in advance for enhanced flavor
and softer cranberries. Serve with blue
tortilla chips or other chips.

Serves 6 to 8

*ALWAYS SUPERB: RECIPES FOR
EVERY OCCASION*
The Junior Leagues of Minneapolis
and St. Paul

Holiday Eggnog

4   egg yolks
1   cup plus 2 tablespoons
     confectioners' sugar
1^1/$_3$ cups apple brandy
2^2/$_3$ cups whipping cream
1^1/$_3$ cups milk
     Ground nutmeg to taste

Beat the egg yolks in a mixer bowl until light. Add the confectioners' sugar, brandy, whipping cream and milk 1 at a time, beating well after each addition. Pour into a punch bowl. Sprinkle with nutmeg.

Makes 1^2/$_3$ quarts

SEABOARD TO SIDEBOARD
The Junior League of Wilmington

🍃 *For variation, whip 2 egg whites in a mixer bowl until stiff peaks form. Fold into the eggnog. The quantity of servings may be changed by increasing the ingredients by half or doubling them. To avoid raw eggs that may carry salmonella, use an equivalent amount or pasteurized egg substitute.*

Spiced Tea

3   cinnamon sticks
14 whole cloves
4   family-size tea bags
2   cups boiling water
1   (4-ounce) package cherry gelatin
1   cup sugar
1/4 cup lemon juice
1   (40-ounce) can pineapple juice
     Water

Combine the cinnamon sticks, cloves and tea bags in a bowl. Pour 2 cups boiling water in the bowl and let steep for 10 minutes. Strain into a 1-gallon stockpot. Add the gelatin and sugar and mix well. Add the lemon juice, pineapple juice and enough water to fill the container. Heat to the desired serving temperature and stir to mix well before serving. Do not refrigerate or the gelatin will set up.

Serves 16

MARVELOUS MORSELS
Maggie Ruth Smith

🍃 *For a gift idea, present this tea in an insulated thermos. Tie with raffia and insert cinnamon sticks into the bow.*

Breakfast & Brunch

There is nothing quite so magical as the hush of dawn on Christmas morning. As kids, we would awaken in the darkness, filled with indescribable delight. Wrapped in fuzzy bathrobes, my brother and sister and I would creep from our warm beds to sneak a peek at the glowing Christmas tree below. We had to keep quiet, as my parents refused to begin Christmas festivities before 6:30 a.m. They also refused to do anything prior to their morning cup of tea.

Never mind waiting on our parents, we decided early on to bring Christmas to them. We made their tea and piled a few slices of Mom's pecan strudel cake on a tray. We gathered the stockings and slowly tiptoed back up the stairs. At 6:30 a.m. on the dot, we burst into my parents' bedroom, announcing the arrival of Christmas. Jumping on their bed with unbridled excitement, we described the marvelous sights below—the presents, the stockings, the glowing lights of the tree in the early morning darkness, the empty plate and glass—Santa had come! "Can we open our stockings now?" we asked hopefully. "We have your tea all ready!" They would laugh, and with mugs in hand, they watched us open our stockings on their big bed.

The magic of Christmas morning has never diminished for me over the years…it has only become more richly layered with meaning. To this day, the stocking tradition has remained. We sleep in a little later now, but my brother and sister and I still get up early and gather the stockings. We still sit on top of my parents' big bed with our cups of coffee or tea and a slice of cake and open our stockings, going around the circle like we've always done. This little ritual has been going on for more than seventeen years, and I couldn't imagine a Christmas morning beginning any other way. Though we will continue to get older, it's the traditions that keep that same magic alive.

ANNA WATSON

Jingle Bell Brunch

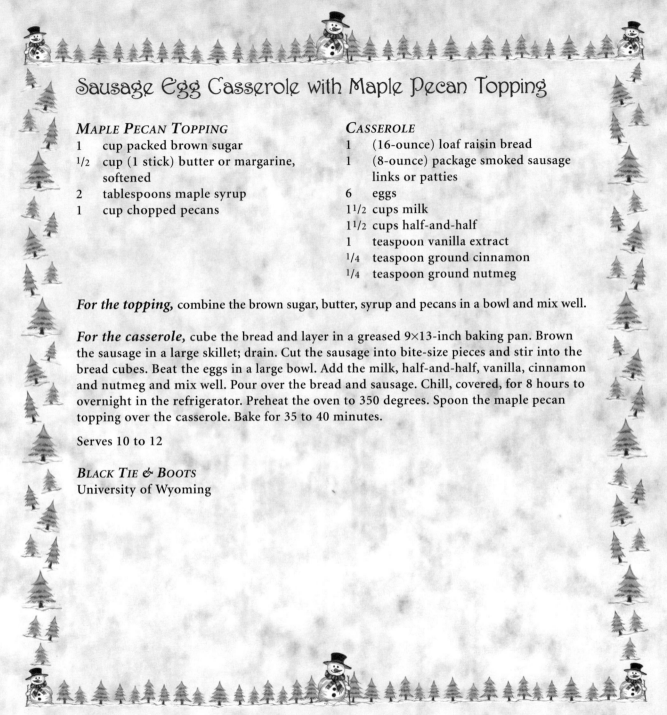

Sausage Egg Casserole with Maple Pecan Topping

MAPLE PECAN TOPPING

1   cup packed brown sugar
1/2 cup (1 stick) butter or margarine, softened
2   tablespoons maple syrup
1   cup chopped pecans

CASSEROLE

1   (16-ounce) loaf raisin bread
1   (8-ounce) package smoked sausage links or patties
6   eggs
1 1/2 cups milk
1 1/2 cups half-and-half
1   teaspoon vanilla extract
1/4 teaspoon ground cinnamon
1/4 teaspoon ground nutmeg

For the topping, combine the brown sugar, butter, syrup and pecans in a bowl and mix well.

For the casserole, cube the bread and layer in a greased 9×13-inch baking pan. Brown the sausage in a large skillet; drain. Cut the sausage into bite-size pieces and stir into the bread cubes. Beat the eggs in a large bowl. Add the milk, half-and-half, vanilla, cinnamon and nutmeg and mix well. Pour over the bread and sausage. Chill, covered, for 8 hours to overnight in the refrigerator. Preheat the oven to 350 degrees. Spoon the maple pecan topping over the casserole. Bake for 35 to 40 minutes.

Serves 10 to 12

BLACK TIE & BOOTS
University of Wyoming

Farmers' Casserole

3   cups frozen shredded hash
brown potatoes
3/4 cup shredded Monterey Jack cheese
with jalapeño chiles, or 3 ounces
shredded Cheddar cheese
1   cup diced cooked ham or
Canadian bacon
1/4 cup sliced green onions
4   eggs, beaten or 1 cup egg substitute
1   (12-ounce) can evaporated milk
1/8 teaspoon salt
1/4 teaspoon pepper

Preheat the oven to 350 degrees. Arrange
the potatoes evenly in a greased 2-quart
baking dish. Sprinkle with the cheese,
ham and green onions. Combine the
eggs, evaporated milk, salt and pepper
in a bowl and mix well. Pour over the
layers. Bake, uncovered, for 40 to
45 minutes or until the center is set.
Let stand for 5 minutes before serving.
You may prepare and chill, covered, for
3 to 12 hours. Uncover and bake for
55 to 60 minutes.

Serves 6

THE BOUNTY OF CHESTER COUNTY
Chester County Agricultural
Development Council

Bacon Tomato Cups

8   slices bacon, cooked and crumbled
1   medium tomato, seeded
and chopped
1/2 small onion, chopped
3   ounces Swiss cheese, shredded
1/2 cup mayonnaise
1   teaspoon basil
1   (10-count) can flaky biscuits

Preheat the oven to 375 degrees.
Combine the bacon, tomato, onion, Swiss
cheese, mayonnaise and basil in a bowl
and mix well. Separate each dough round
into 3 layers. Press one layer into each
miniature muffin cup. Spoon the filling
into each cup. Bake for 10 to 12 minutes
or until the edges are brown.

Makes 30 miniature muffins

SETTINGS ON THE DOCK OF THE BAY
Assistance League of the Bay Area

*The filling can be prepared 1 day
in advance and refrigerated until ready
to use.*

Herbed Sausage Puffs

2 (12-ounce) packages bulk pork sausage, 1 regular and 1 hot
1 cup (4 ounces) grated Swiss cheese
1 tablespoon grated Parmesan cheese
3 eggs, well beaten
1 tablespoon dried or fresh parsley flakes
1 tablespoon dried or fresh basil leaves, crushed
1 teaspoon garlic powder
Salt and pepper to taste
1 (18-ounce) package frozen puff pastry, thawed
1/2 cup Dijon mustard
2 tablespoons honey

Brown the sausage in a large skillet; drain and set aside to cool. Add the cheeses, all but 2 tablespoons of the eggs and the seasonings to the sausage and stir gently.

Preheat the oven to 350 degrees. Keep the pastry very cold until ready to use. Roll out one sheet of pastry to a 12×17-inch rectangle. Place half the sausage mixture along one side of the rectangle. Bring the sides together by rolling over. Pinch the ends tightly. Repeat with the remaining pastry and sausage mixture.

Place on a baking sheet and form a semi-circle. Brush with the reserved egg. Bake for 30 to 40 minutes or until golden brown. Remove from the oven and cool for 10 minutes. Cut into 1 1/2-inch slices.

Combine the Dijon mustard and honey in a bowl and mix well. Serve with the sausage puffs.

Serves 6 to 8

OF TIDE AND THYME
The Junior League of Annapolis

The puffs can be frozen once formed. Remove from the freezer and let thaw before baking.

Speck and Dicken

1	pound ground beef
1	pound bulk pork sausage
4	eggs
4	cups buttermilk
1	cup dark corn syrup
5^{1}/2	cups all-purpose flour
2	cups packed brown sugar
^{1}/2	cup granulated sugar
2	teaspoons baking soda
2	teaspoons salt

Combine the ground beef and sausage in a bowl and mix well. Shape into very thin patties no larger than 2 inches in diameter. Arrange on waxed paper and chill in the refrigerator until ready to use.

Preheat a lightly greased griddle. Combine the eggs, buttermilk, corn syrup, flour, brown sugar, granulated sugar, baking soda and salt in a large bowl and mix well. Arrange the meat patties 6 inches apart on the griddle. Cook until brown on 1 side. Turn the patties over and pour batter over each. Do not allow more than 1^{1}/2 inches of batter to run beyond the edge of the patties. Cook until the batter begins to bubble. Turn and cook until the pancakes are golden brown. Serve with applesauce or maple syrup.

Serves about 8

FURNITURE CITY FEASTS RESTORED
The Junior League of High Point

This German dish is traditionally eaten on New Year's Eve. Legend has it that the more you can eat before midnight, the more money you will receive in the upcoming year. However, if you eat even a bite after midnight, it will bring you bad luck!

Sautéed Shrimp and Peppers over Cheese Grits

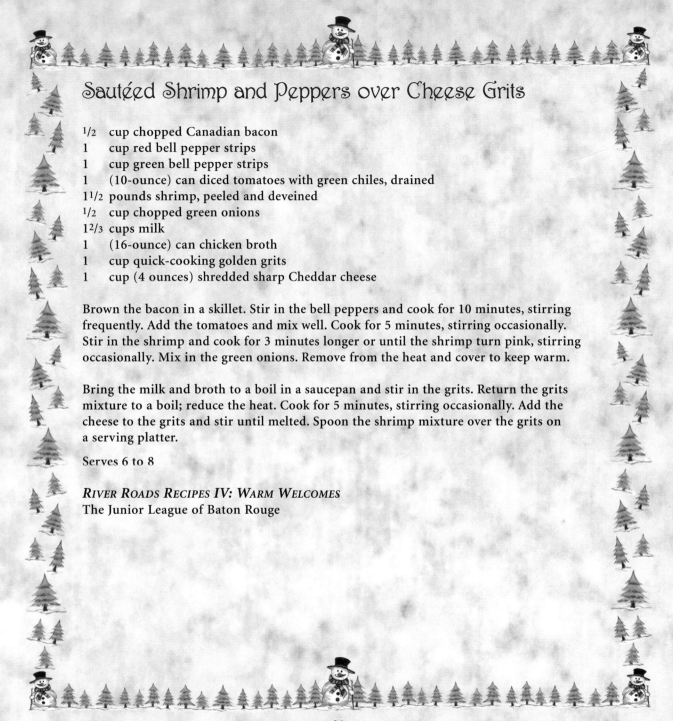

1/2   cup chopped Canadian bacon
1   cup red bell pepper strips
1   cup green bell pepper strips
1   (10-ounce) can diced tomatoes with green chiles, drained
1 1/2 pounds shrimp, peeled and deveined
1/2   cup chopped green onions
1 2/3 cups milk
1   (16-ounce) can chicken broth
1   cup quick-cooking golden grits
1   cup (4 ounces) shredded sharp Cheddar cheese

Brown the bacon in a skillet. Stir in the bell peppers and cook for 10 minutes, stirring frequently. Add the tomatoes and mix well. Cook for 5 minutes, stirring occasionally. Stir in the shrimp and cook for 3 minutes longer or until the shrimp turn pink, stirring occasionally. Mix in the green onions. Remove from the heat and cover to keep warm.

Bring the milk and broth to a boil in a saucepan and stir in the grits. Return the grits mixture to a boil; reduce the heat. Cook for 5 minutes, stirring occasionally. Add the cheese to the grits and stir until melted. Spoon the shrimp mixture over the grits on a serving platter.

Serves 6 to 8

RIVER ROADS RECIPES IV: WARM WELCOMES
The Junior League of Baton Rouge

Potato and Leek Tart

PASTRY
1¼ cups flour
½ teaspoon salt
½ cup (1 stick) chilled butter, cut into small pieces
2 to 3 tablespoons ice water

FILLING
3 tablespoons butter
3 large leeks, trimmed and thinly sliced
3 tablespoons whipping cream
¼ teaspoon ground nutmeg
¼ teaspoon salt
⅛ teaspoon pepper
1 large russet potato, cooked, peeled and thinly sliced

For the pastry, mix the flour and salt in a medium bowl. Cut in the butter with a pastry blender or 2 forks until crumbly. Add the water 1 tablespoons at a time, tossing with a fork until a soft dough forms. Shape into a ball. Chill, wrapped in plastic wrap, for 1 hour. Roll the dough into an 11-inch circle on a floured surface. Fit the pastry into a 9-inch quiche pan or pie plate. Trim the pastry even with the edge of the pan. Chill for 30 minutes. Preheat the oven to 375 degrees. Prick the pastry with a fork. Line with foil and fill with pie weights or dried beans. Bake for 10 minutes. Remove the foil and weights. Bake for 10 minutes longer or until the crust is firm. Cool on a wire rack. You may use a purchased prepared pie crust in this recipe or your own favorite pastry recipe.

For the filling, melt the butter in a large skillet over medium heat. Add the leeks. Cook for 10 minutes or until tender. Remove and reserve 1 cup leeks. Stir the whipping cream, nutmeg, salt and pepper into the remaining leeks in the skillet. Cook for 2 minutes or until thickened, stirring occasionally. Increase the oven temperature to 400 degrees. Spoon the filling into the crust. Top with the potato slices and reserved leeks, arranging the potatoes in the center and the leeks at the edge. Bake for 10 to 15 minutes or until the filling is heated through. Cool slightly on a wire rack.

Makes 10 appetizer servings or 6 brunch entrée servings

BEYOND BURLAP
The Junior League of Boise

Vegetable Quiches

1   small package chopped
     fresh mushrooms
1   onion, chopped
3/4   green bell pepper, chopped
     Vegetable oil for sautéing
4   eggs, beaten
7   ounces half-and-half
6   ounces Cheddar cheese, shredded
6   ounces mozzarella cheese, shredded
2   unbaked (9-inch) pie shells

Preheat the oven to 350 degrees. Sauté the mushrooms, onion and green pepper in a small amount of vegetable oil until tender. Combine the eggs and half-and-half in a large bowl and mix will. Stir in the sautéed vegetables, Cheddar cheese and mozzarella cheese. Pour into the pie shells. Bake for 35 to 45 minutes or until the top is golden brown and the center is firm. Let cool for 10 minutes before serving.

Serves 12 to 16

SEABOARD TO SIDEBOARD
The Junior League of Wilmington

Grits Galore

4   cups water
1 1/3   cups milk
1 1/2   cups quick-cooking grits
4   ounces cream cheese
1   cup (4 ounces) shredded
     Cheddar cheese
8   slices bacon, crisp-cooked
     and crumbled
1   (10-ounce) can tomatoes with
     green chiles
     Additional crumbled cooked bacon
     for garnish

Combine the water and milk in a 2-quart saucepan. Bring to a boil and stir in the grits. Return to a boil. Reduce the heat and cover. Simmer for 5 to 7 minutes, adding more water if needed.

Add the cream cheese and Cheddar cheese. Cook until the cheese melt, stirring constantly. Stir in the bacon and tomatoes with green chiles. Spoon into a serving bowl and garnish with crumbled bacon. Serve immediately.

Serves 6 to 8

PAR 3 TEA TIME AT THE MASTERS®
The Junior League of Augusta

Sticky Potato Buns

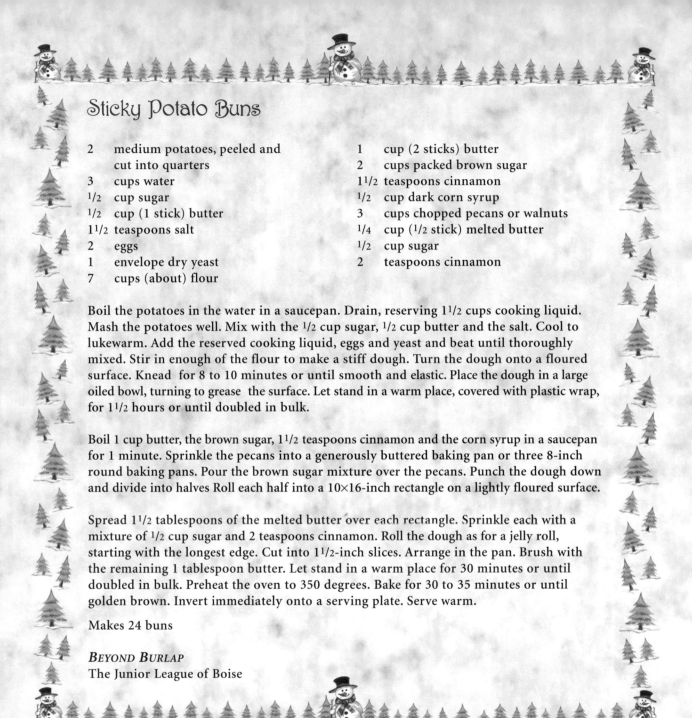

2	medium potatoes, peeled and cut into quarters	1	cup (2 sticks) butter
3	cups water	2	cups packed brown sugar
1/2	cup sugar	1 1/2	teaspoons cinnamon
1/2	cup (1 stick) butter	1/2	cup dark corn syrup
1 1/2	teaspoons salt	3	cups chopped pecans or walnuts
2	eggs	1/4	cup (1/2 stick) melted butter
1	envelope dry yeast	1/2	cup sugar
7	cups (about) flour	2	teaspoons cinnamon

Boil the potatoes in the water in a saucepan. Drain, reserving 1 1/2 cups cooking liquid. Mash the potatoes well. Mix with the 1/2 cup sugar, 1/2 cup butter and the salt. Cool to lukewarm. Add the reserved cooking liquid, eggs and yeast and beat until thoroughly mixed. Stir in enough of the flour to make a stiff dough. Turn the dough onto a floured surface. Knead for 8 to 10 minutes or until smooth and elastic. Place the dough in a large oiled bowl, turning to grease the surface. Let stand in a warm place, covered with plastic wrap, for 1 1/2 hours or until doubled in bulk.

Boil 1 cup butter, the brown sugar, 1 1/2 teaspoons cinnamon and the corn syrup in a saucepan for 1 minute. Sprinkle the pecans into a generously buttered baking pan or three 8-inch round baking pans. Pour the brown sugar mixture over the pecans. Punch the dough down and divide into halves Roll each half into a 10×16-inch rectangle on a lightly floured surface.

Spread 1 1/2 tablespoons of the melted butter over each rectangle. Sprinkle each with a mixture of 1/2 cup sugar and 2 teaspoons cinnamon. Roll the dough as for a jelly roll, starting with the longest edge. Cut into 1 1/2-inch slices. Arrange in the pan. Brush with the remaining 1 tablespoon butter. Let stand in a warm place for 30 minutes or until doubled in bulk. Preheat the oven to 350 degrees. Bake for 30 to 35 minutes or until golden brown. Invert immediately onto a serving plate. Serve warm.

Makes 24 buns

BEYOND BURLAP
The Junior League of Boise

Orange Rosemary Scones

2	cups flour
1/4	cup sugar
1	tablespoon baking powder
1/4	teaspoon salt
2	or 3 sprigs of rosemary, snipped
1/3	cup butter, chilled and cubed
1/4	cup half-and-half
1/4	cup fresh orange juice
1	egg, beaten
2	tablespoons grated orange zest
1	tablespoon half-and-half
1	tablespoon fresh orange juice
1	tablespoon sugar

Preheat the oven to 350 degrees. Combine the flour, 1/4 cup sugar, baking powder, salt and rosemary in a bowl and mix well. Cut in the butter with a pastry blender until crumbly. Mix 1/4 cup half-and-half, 1/4 cup orange juice, egg and orange zest in a bowl. Add the orange juice mixture to the crumb mixture and stir with a fork just until moistened.

Shape the dough into a ball. Pat into an 8-inch circle on an ungreased baking sheet. Score into 8 wedges using a sharp knife. Brush the top with a mixture of 1 tablespoon half-and-half, 1 tablespoon orange juice and 1 tablespoon sugar. Bake for 25 minutes. Serve warm.

Makes 8 scones

RIVER ROAD RECIPES IV: WARM WELCOMES
The Junior League of Baton Rouge

Cherry Almond Twist Pastry

1   package (3 ounces) dried cherries (about 2/3 cup)
1   package (7 to 8 ounces) almond paste (not marzipan)
1/4 cup (1/2 stick) butter, softened
1   box (17.3 ounces) frozen puff pastry sheets, thawed
1   egg, beaten with 1 teaspoon water
1/4 cup sliced almonds (optional)

Place the dried cherries in a small bowl with just enough hot water to cover. Let stand for 3 to 5 minutes. Drain; set aside. In the work bowl of a food processor fitted with a steel knife blade, process the almond paste and butter until smooth. Add the cherries; pulse just until the cherries are evenly mixed (the cherries should still be chunky).

Preheat the oven to 400 degrees. On a lightly floured surface, roll one of the pastry sheets into an 11-inch square. Place on a parchment-lined baking sheet. With a sharp knife or pizza cutter, trim the corners to form an 11-inch circle. Spread the almond filling evenly over the pastry, leaving a 1/2-inch border around the edges. Roll a second sheet of pastry into an 11-inch square. Place over the filling. Trim to fit the bottom layer; seal the edges. Lightly press a 1 1/2-inch round biscuit cutter in the center of the pastry to form a guideline. Cut the pastry into 16 equal wedges, cutting just to the edge of the center circle. (Wedges should be about 1 1/2 inches wide at the outside edge. Give each wedge a double twist, forming a starburst pattern. Brush the egg mixture over the pastry. If desired, sprinkle almonds over the top. Bake until the pastry is golden brown and puffed, about 20 minutes. Cool slightly. Best served warm.

Serves 8 to 10

THE BEST OF DIERBERGS
Dierbergs Markets, Inc.

For best results, assemble the pastry just before baking. If desired, prepare the cherry almond filling and refrigerate up to 24 hours. Assemble the pastry as directed.

Cinnamon Roll-Ups

24   slices firm white sandwich bread,
     crusts removed
8   ounces cream cheese, softened
1   egg yolk
1 1/4 cups sugar
1   tablespoon cinnamon
1/2 cup (1 stick) unsalted butter, melted

Roll the bread slices flat with a rolling
pin or press with hands. Mix the cream
cheese, egg yolk and 1/4 cup of the sugar
in a bowl. Spread about 1 tablespoon on
each bread slice and roll up tightly. Mix
the remaining sugar and the cinnamon
in a shallow bowl. Brush each roll-up
with the melted butter and roll in the
cinnamon-sugar. Arrange on a baking
sheet. Chill or freeze for at least 2 hours.
Preheat the oven to 400 degrees. Bake for
9 to 12 minutes or until golden brown.
Serve warm.

Serves 12

PAR 3 TEA TIME AT THE MASTERS®
The Junior League of Augusta

*These can be frozen for up to two
months before baking.*

Honey Puff

3   ounces cream cheese, cubed
     and softened
1   cup flour
1   cup milk
6   eggs
3   tablespoons honey
1   teaspoon vanilla extract
1/2 teaspoon salt
1/2 teaspoon baking powder
3   tablespoons butter
2   tablespoons confectioners' sugar
     Fresh seasonal fruit

Preheat the oven to 375 degrees. Combine
the cream cheese, flour, milk, eggs, honey,
vanilla, salt and baking powder in a blender
container. Process on High for 2 to
4 minutes or until blended. Heat the butter
in a 10-inch ovenproof skillet or baking pan
in the oven until melted. Pour the cream
cheese mixture into the prepared skillet or
baking pan. Bake for 25 to 30 minutes or
until a knife inserted in the middle comes
out clean. Sprinkle with the confectioners'
sugar. Garnish with seasonal fruit. Note:
The puff will rise and fall like a soufflé.

Serves 6

TEXAS TIES
The Junior League of North Harris and
South Montgomery Counties

Blueberry French Toast Bake

BLUEBERRY FRENCH TOAST

9 cups French bread cubes
8 ounces cream cheese, cubed
8 ounces fresh or thawed frozen
   blueberries
2 cups milk
6 eggs
1 teaspoon vanilla extract
1/4 cup (1/2 stick) butter, melted
1/3 cup maple-flavored syrup
   Cinnamon to taste

BROWN SUGAR SYRUP

1 cup packed brown sugar
1 cup heavy cream
1 cup light corn syrup
   Salt to taste

To prepare the French toast, sprinkle half the bread cubes in a greased 2-quart baking dish. Add the cream cheese cubes and blueberries. Top with the remaining bread cubes. Combine the milk, eggs and vanilla in a bowl and mix well. Pour over the layers in the baking dish and press down lightly to saturate the bread with the liquid. Combine the butter and syrup in a bowl and mix well. Pour over the layers and sprinkle lightly with cinnamon. Chill the mixture, covered, for 2 hours or longer. Preheat the oven to 325 degrees. Bake for 30 to 40 minutes or until golden brown and set.

To prepare the syrup, combine the brown sugar, cream, corn syrup and salt in a small saucepan. Cook over low heat until smooth, stirring to blend well; do not boil. Serve with the French toast. You may microwave the syrup if preferred.

Serves 10

BEACH APPÉTIT
The Junior League of the Emerald Coast

Oven French Toast

4	eggs
2/3	cup frozen orange juice concentrate, thawed
1/3	cup milk
3/4	cup sugar
1/2	teaspoon vanilla extract
1/4	teaspoon nutmeg
1/4	teaspoon cinnamon
8	(1/2-inch) slices French bread
1/4	cup (1/2 stick) margarine, melted
1/2	cup (1 stick) margarine
1/2	cup sugar
1/2	cup orange juice

Combine the eggs, orange juice concentrate, milk, 3/4 cup sugar, vanilla, nutmeg and cinnamon in a bowl and mix well. Grease a 9×13-inch baking pan lightly. Arrange the bread in the prepared pan.

Pour the egg mixture evenly over the bread. Chill, covered, for 8 to 12 hours. Let stand at room temperature for 30 to 45 minutes. Drizzle with the melted margarine. Preheat the oven to350 degrees. Bake for 30 minutes or until light brown.

Combine 1/2 cup margarine, 1/2 cup sugar and the orange juice in a microwave-safe bowl. Microwave until bubbly, stirring occasionally. Serve over the French toast.

Serves 6

As Always
Norma Fleming Murray

Cranberry Streusel Coffee Cake

CAKE
1/2 cup (1 stick) unsalted butter, at room temperature
1 cup granulated sugar
2 large eggs
1 teaspoon vanilla extract
1 tablespoon grated orange zest
2 cups unbleached all-purpose flour
1 teaspoon baking powder
1 teaspoon baking soda
1/2 teaspoon salt
1 cup sour cream
2 1/2 cups whole fresh cranberries

TOPPING
3/4 cup packed light brown sugar
1/2 cup unbleached all-purpose flour
2 1/2 teaspoons cinnamon
1/4 cup (1/2 stick) unsalted butter
1/2 cup walnuts, chopped (optional)

For the cake, preheat the oven to 350 degrees. Grease and flour a 9×13-inch baking pan. Using an electric mixer, cream the butter and sugar together until light and fluffy. Beat in the eggs one at a time, then add the vanilla and orange zest. Mix the flour, baking powder, soda and salt together. Add the flour mixture to the creamed mixture, alternating with the sour cream to make a smooth, thick batter. Spread the batter evenly in the prepared pan. Sprinkle the cranberries over the top.

For the topping, in a small mixing bowl, toss the sugar, flour and cinnamon together. Cut in the butter with 2 knives or a pastry blender until the mixture is crumbly. Stir in the walnuts. Sprinkle the streusel evenly over the cranberries on the coffee cake.

Bake for 45 minutes, or until a tester inserted in the center comes out clean. Cut into squares and serve warm or at room temperature.

Serves 10

MAD ABOUT FOOD
The Junior League of Madison

Merk's Coffee Cake

2   cups sifted flour
1   teaspoon baking powder
1   teaspoon baking soda
3/4   cup sugar
1/2   cup shortening
1   teaspoon vanilla extract
3   eggs
1   cup sour cream
1   cup packed brown sugar
6   tablespoons butter or margarine, softened
2   teaspoons cinnamon
1   cup chopped nuts

Preheat the oven to 350 degrees. Grease a 10-inch tube pan; line the bottom with waxed paper. Sift the flour, baking powder and baking soda together. Beat the sugar, shortening and vanilla in a mixer bowl until creamy, scraping the bowl occasionally. Add the eggs 1 at a time, beating well after each addition. Add the dry ingredients alternately with the sour cream, mixing after each addition. Spread 1/2 of the batter in the prepared tube pan.

Beat the brown sugar, butter and cinnamon in a mixer bowl until creamy, scraping the bowl occasionally. Stir in the nuts. Dot 1/2 of the nut mixture over the prepared layer. Spread with the remaining batter. Dot with the remaining nut mixture. Bake for 50 minutes or until the coffee cake tests done.

Serves 16

GREAT LAKES EFFECTS
The Junior League of Buffalo

Real Moravian Sugar Cake

1   envelope dry yeast (not instant)
1/2 cup lukewarm water
1   cup hot unseasoned mashed potatoes (made from fresh potatoes;
     1 cup potato cooking water reserved)
1   cup granulated sugar
1/2 cup shortening
1/4 cup (1/2 stick) butter, softened
1   teaspoon salt
2   eggs, beaten
3   cups all-purpose flour
     Additional butter, softened
     Brown sugar and ground cinnamon
     Heavy cream or whipping cream

Dissolve the yeast in the water in a small bowl. Combine the mashed potatoes, granulated sugar, shortening, 1/4 cup butter and the salt in a large bowl and mix well. Cool to lukewarm. Add the yeast mixture and reserved potato water and mix well. Cover and let rise until spongy. Add the eggs. Add the flour 1/2 cup at a time, stirring to make a soft dough. Do not knead. Let rise until doubled in bulk. Punch down and divide the dough in half. Spread each half in a greased 10×15-inch cake pan and let rise. Preheat the oven to 375 degrees. Make indentations in the dough with your fingers. Fill the indentations with softened butter and brown sugar. Sprinkle with cinnamon and drizzle with cream. Bake for 20 minutes. Serve warm.

Serves 24 to 30

FURNITURE CITY FEASTS RESTORED
The Junior League of High Point

Moravian Sugar Cake is traditionally eaten for breakfast, but it is equally as good as a dessert after a Christmas meal. And it is always best eaten fresh from the oven.

B and B Baked Oatmeal

6	cups quick-cooking or old-fashioned oats
1	tablespoon plus 1 teaspoon baking powder
1	teaspoon salt
1	teaspoon cinnamon
1	cup vegetable oil
1 1/2	cups packed brown sugar
4	eggs
2	cups milk
1	cup chopped apple (optional)
1	cup raisins (optional)
1/2	cups flaked coconut (optional)

Preheat the oven to 400 degrees. Combine the oats, baking powder, salt and cinnamon in a bowl and mix well. Combine the oil, brown sugar and eggs in a separate bowl and mix well. Stir in the dry ingredients. Stir in the milk, apple, raisins and coconut. Pour into a greased 9×13-inch baking dish, spreading evenly. Bake for 30 to 35 minutes. Cut into squares. Serve warm with milk or cream.

Serves 15

PICNICS, POTLUCKS & PRIZEWINNERS
Indiana 4-H Foundation

Served at a popular Hoosier B & B, this hearty baked oatmeal is a great choice for Christmas morning breakfast or a leisurely brunch. Prepare and refrigerate this homey dish the day before and then just pop into the oven while the kids are opening their gifts. Instead of apples, raisins and coconut, add dried apricots or dates and chopped pecans. For a special touch, drizzle each serving with maple syrup before passing the milk or cream.

Holiday Apples

2   (29-ounce) cans Comstock apples, unsweetened with juice
4   cups bread cubes with crust
1   cup margarine
$3/4$ cup sugar
$3/4$ cup packed brown sugar
$1/2$ teaspoon nutmeg
$3/4$ teaspoon cinnamon
$1/2$ cup apple juice
$1/8$ cup lemon juice

Preheat the oven to 350 degrees. Combine the apples, bread cubes, margarine, sugar, brown sugar, nutmeg, cinnamon, apple juice and lemon juice in a bowl and mix well. Spoon into a 2-quart or 9×13-inch baking pan. Bake for 45 minutes.

Serves 12

GEORGIA ON MY MENU
The Junior League of Cobb-Marietta

Mandarin Fruit Salad

1   (11-ounce) can mandarin oranges, drained
1   (8-ounce) can pineapple tidbits, drained
1   (4-ounce) can flaked coconut
1   cup miniature marshmallows
$1/2$ to 1 small bottle maraschino cherries, drained and quartered
    White seedless grapes, cut into halves
1   cup sour cream

Combine the mandarin oranges, pineapple, coconut, marshmallows, cherries, grapes and sour cream in a bowl and mix gently. Chill, covered, for 24 hours before serving.

Serves 4 to 6

RALPH AND DONNA McDONALD

Simple Fruit Salad

2   (15-ounce) cans pineapple chunks
1   (11-ounce) can mandarin
     oranges, drained
3   bananas, sliced
1   (3-ounce) package vanilla instant
     pudding mix
3   tablespoons orange breakfast
     drink mix
     Chopped nuts to taste
     Miniature marshmallows to taste

Drain the pineapple and reserve the juice. Combine the pineapple, mandarin oranges and bananas in a bowl. Sprinkle the pudding mix over the fruit.

Combine the reserved pineapple juice and orange breakfast drink mix in a small bowl and mix well. Pour the pineapple juice mixture over the fruit and mix well. Fold in chopped nuts and marshmallows. Chill, covered, until serving time.

Serves 4 to 6

MARVELOUS MORSELS
Maggie Ruth Smith

Christmas Fruit Punch

2   cups cranberry juice
2   cups pineapple juice
1   (6-ounce) can frozen lemonade
     concentrate, thawed
1   (6-ounce) can frozen orange juice
     concentrate, thawed
1   (10-ounce) package frozen sweetened
     strawberries or raspberries, thawed
1   large lime, sliced
4   cups ginger ale, chilled
30 ice cubes

Combine the cranberry juice, pineapple juice, lemonade concentrate, orange juice concentrate, strawberries and lime slices in a large bowl and mix well. Refrigerate until completely chilled. Pour into a punch bowl. Stir in the ginger ale and ice cubes.

Makes 32 ($1/2$-cup) servings

PICNICS, POTLUCKS & PRIZEWINNERS
Indiana 4-H Foundation

Christmas Dinner

Christmas Eve in Italian families is a very special occasion. Ours is no exception. My first memories are of my grandmother inviting the entire family—her father, sons, sisters and their families, and assorted relatives—to her home for an especially festive Christmas Eve party. Everyone looked forward to the occasion: adults for one reason; children for another; and Grandma for all of them. As a young child, I remember my grandmother and her sister spending the entire day making homemade ravioli and placing huge sheet pans full of them on all of the beds in the house to store until ready to cook. When I was old enough, my father would drop me off at Grandma's to spend the day "helping."

Over the years, the crowd changed in size and variation of relatives, but one thing was evidently clear: everyone cherished this Christmas Eve celebration of family love. I still remember my grandmother peeking out of her kitchen in her Christmas apron waving to my father's 8 mm home movie camera with a very proud smile on her face. Unfortunately, Grandma is no longer with us, but my mother and father continue these memorable Christmas Eve celebrations at the house in which I grew up. My siblings and I truly look forward to seeing each other on this occasion, as it becomes harder and harder to get together throughout the year. Mom insists on doing all the work herself in spite of our desire to assist. It is now her holiday with all the traditions and the love that accompany it. My father is all smiles. He also proudly presents my mother with the annual Christmas corsage, just as Grandma wore. Mom's family-famous meatballs are the new "raviolis."

It is for these reasons that I have learned to love family holidays and hosting some of them at my own home. I don't think of it as work, but as a gift that I am giving my loved ones—the gift of family love. It is both a blessing and a practical Christmas present that you can give every day.

BARBARA SEELIG BROWN

Merry Christmas Dinner

Chestnut Soup   page 49
or St. Catherine's Oyster Bisque   page 50

Pear, Arugula and Endive Salad with Candied Walnuts   page 52

Beef Brisket with Portabella Mushrooms and Dried Cherries   page 53
or Annapolis Stuffed Pork Roast   page 55
or Cornish Game Hens with Blackberry Honey   page 59

Carrot and Sweet Potato Purée   page 63

Company Peas   page 65

Garlic Mashed Potatoes   page 66
or Corn Bread Dressing   page 70

Spinach Madeleine   page 67

The Official Miss Forbus' Squash Casserole   page 66
or Surprise Corn Pudding   page 64

Fresh Cranberry Apple Relish   page 69

Foolproof Homemade Yeast Rolls   page 71

Cranberry Marsh Ice   page 79 and
Lemon and White Chocolate Shortbread   page 96
or White Chocolate Mousse Torte   page 77

Chestnut Soup

2	tablespoons butter		4	cups canned low-salt chicken broth
1	tablespoon olive oil		2	cups boiled chestnuts, or 2 cups
1	celery stalk, chopped			(10 ounces) vacuum-packed
1	small carrot, chopped			chestnuts, halved
1/2	onion, chopped			Salt and pepper
1	teaspoon minced fresh thyme, or		1/4	cup whipping cream
	1/4 teaspoon dried thyme			Pinch of salt

Melt the butter with the oil in a heavy large saucepan over medium heat. Add the celery, carrot, onion and thyme and sauté until the vegetables are tender, about 10 minutes. Add the broth and chestnuts. Cover partially and simmer until the chestnuts are very tender, about 30 minutes. Purée the soup in batches in a blender. Season to taste with salt and pepper. Can be prepared 1 day ahead. Cover and chill.

Whisk the cream and a pinch of salt in a medium bowl until thickened but not stiff. Bring the soup to a simmer over low heat. Ladle into bowls. Swirl a spoonful of cream into each bowl and serve.

Serves 4

MAD ABOUT FOOD
The Junior League of Madison

To boil chestnuts, use a small sharp knife to cut an "x" in each chestnut. Cook the chestnuts in a large saucepan of boiling water for 15 minutes or just until tender. Transfer the chestnuts to a work surface. Remove and discard the hard shell and papery brown skin while the chestnuts are still warm.

St. Catherine's Oyster Bisque

1 quart oysters	1/4 cup flour
1 pint oysters (optional)	Nutmeg to taste
Salt and pepper to taste	Dash of curry powder
4 ribs celery, chopped	Dash of MSG
1 medium onion, chopped	1 tablespoon lemon juice
4 cups milk	1 tablespoon Worcestershire sauce
2 cups whipping cream	Red pepper to taste
1/4 cup (1/2 stick) butter	

Drain the oysters and remove any shells. Combine the oysters with salt and pepper in a saucepan. Simmer, covered, over low heat until the edges begin to curl, stirring occasionally. Drain the oysters, reserving the stock. Strain the stock into a bowl. Cook the celery and onion in water in a saucepan until tender. Drain, reserving the liquid. Pour the reserved liquid into the oyster stock. Stir the milk and 1³/4 cups of the whipping cream into the oyster stock.

Heat the butter in a saucepan until melted. Stir in the flour. Add the milk mixture, whisking constantly. Cook until smooth and thickened, stirring constantly. Stir in nutmeg, curry, MSG, the lemon juice, Worcestershire sauce and red pepper. Adjust the seasonings to taste. Grind the cooked oysters, onion and celery in a grinder. Keep warm over hot water until ready to serve. Whip the remaining 1/4 cup whipping cream in a mixer bowl. Combine the ground oyster mixture with the bisque and mix well. Ladle into soup bowls. Top with a dollop of whipped cream. Garnish with paprika and chopped parsley.

Serves 6

FROM BLACK TIE TO BLACKEYED PEAS
Dr. Victor Irving

Balsamic Bermuda Onion Salad

ONIONS

1/4 cup olive oil
1/4 cup balsamic vinegar
1 teaspoon kosher salt
1/2 teaspoon pepper
3 small red onions, cut into rings
2 tablespoons balsamic vinegar

SALAD

6 tablespoons minced shallots
2 teaspoons Dijon mustard
1/4 cup red wine vinegar
1/2 teaspoon kosher salt
1/2 teaspoon pepper
3/4 cup olive oil
2 heads red leaf lettuce, torn

For the onions, preheat the oven to 375 degrees. Whisk the olive oil, 1/4 cup balsamic vinegar, salt and pepper in a bowl. Add the onion rings and toss to coat. Spoon into a baking dish. Bake for 15 minutes. Sprinkle with 2 tablespoons balsamic vinegar; let cool.

For the salad, whisk the shallots, Dijon mustard, red wine vinegar, salt and pepper in a large bowl. Whisk in the olive oil slowly. Add the lettuce just before serving and toss to coat. Arrange the salad on salad plates and top with the onion rings.

Serves 10 to 12

PAR 3 TEA TIME AT THE MASTERS®
The Junior League of Augusta

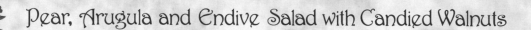

Pear, Arugula and Endive Salad with Candied Walnuts

CANDIED WALNUTS
Nonstick vegetable oil spray
1 cup walnuts
2 tablespoons light corn syrup
1 tablespoon sugar
1/2 teaspoon salt
1/4 teaspoon ground black pepper
1 tablespoon brown sugar
1/8 teaspoon cayenne pepper

SALAD
2 tablespoons red wine vinegar
2 tablespoons fresh lemon juice
1 tablespoon chopped fresh parsley

2 teaspoons Dijon mustard
6 tablespoons walnut oil or olive oil
6 tablespoons extra-virgin olive oil
Salt and pepper
12 cups (about 12 ounces) arugula, torn into pieces
4 heads Belgian endive, trimmed and leaves separated
2 firm but ripe pears, halved, cored and thinly sliced lengthwise
1 cup feta cheese

For the walnuts, preheat the oven to 325 degrees. Spray a baking sheet with nonstick spray. Combine the walnuts and the remaining ingredients in a medium bowl and toss to coat. Spread the nut mixture on the prepared baking sheet. Some nuts may clump together. Bake for 15 minutes, stirring occasionally to break up any clumps, until the nuts are deep golden and the sugar mixture is bubbling. Cool completely on the baking sheet. Can be made 3 days ahead. Store in an airtight container.

For the salad, whisk together the vinegar, lemon juice, parsley and mustard in a medium bowl. Add the walnut oil and olive oil and whisk until well blended. Season the dressing to taste with salt and pepper. Can be made 1 day ahead. Cover and chill. Let stand at room temperature for 1 hour and re-whisk before continuing. Toss the arugula in a large bowl with enough dressing to coat. Divide the dressed arugula among 10 plates. Arrange the endive leaves and pear slices atop the arugula on each plate. Drizzle with additional dressing. Sprinkle with the candied walnuts and serve.

Serves 10

MAD ABOUT FOOD
The Junior League of Madison

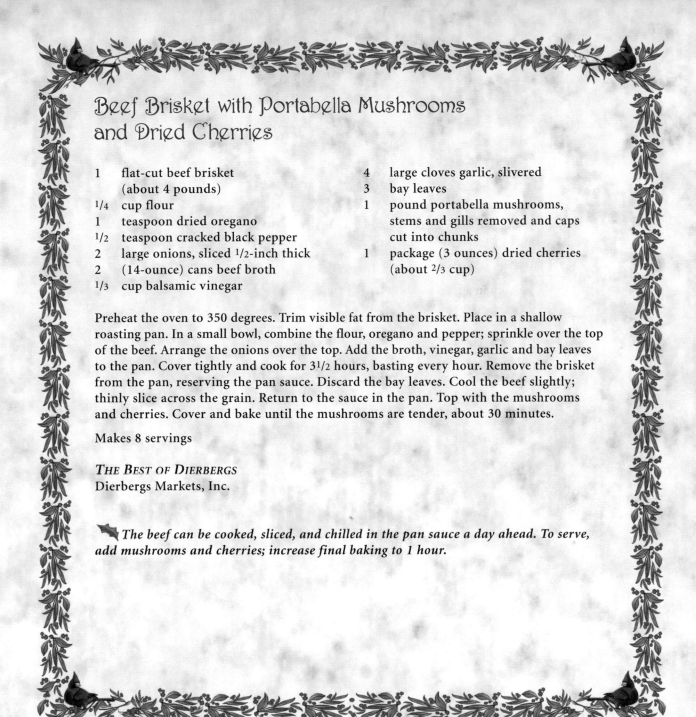

Beef Brisket with Portabella Mushrooms and Dried Cherries

1	flat-cut beef brisket (about 4 pounds)
1/4	cup flour
1	teaspoon dried oregano
1/2	teaspoon cracked black pepper
2	large onions, sliced 1/2-inch thick
2	(14-ounce) cans beef broth
1/3	cup balsamic vinegar

4	large cloves garlic, slivered
3	bay leaves
1	pound portabella mushrooms, stems and gills removed and caps cut into chunks
1	package (3 ounces) dried cherries (about 2/3 cup)

Preheat the oven to 350 degrees. Trim visible fat from the brisket. Place in a shallow roasting pan. In a small bowl, combine the flour, oregano and pepper; sprinkle over the top of the beef. Arrange the onions over the top. Add the broth, vinegar, garlic and bay leaves to the pan. Cover tightly and cook for 3 1/2 hours, basting every hour. Remove the brisket from the pan, reserving the pan sauce. Discard the bay leaves. Cool the beef slightly; thinly slice across the grain. Return to the sauce in the pan. Top with the mushrooms and cherries. Cover and bake until the mushrooms are tender, about 30 minutes.

Makes 8 servings

THE BEST OF DIERBERGS
Dierbergs Markets, Inc.

The beef can be cooked, sliced, and chilled in the pan sauce a day ahead. To serve, add mushrooms and cherries; increase final baking to 1 hour.

Herb-Marinated Lamb

1	(5- to 6-pound) leg of lamb, butterflied
1/2	cup olive oil
1/2	cup lemon juice
1/4	cup chopped onion
3	garlic cloves, minced
1	tablespoon Worcestershire sauce
1/2	teaspoon ground pepper
1/2	teaspoon dried thyme

Place the leg of lamb in a nonreactive dish. Combine the olive oil, lemon juice, onion, garlic, Worcestershire sauce, pepper and thyme in a bowl and mix well. Pour over the lamb, turning to coat. Marinate in the refrigerator for 3 to 10 hours, turning occasionally. Drain, reserving the marinade.

Grill the lamb over hot coals for 40 to 45 minutes or until done to taste, basting with the reserved marinade occasionally.

Makes 12 to 15 servings

GREAT LAKES EFFECTS
The Junior League of Buffalo

Annapolis Stuffed Pork Roast

1	(3¹/₂ pound) boned center loin pork roast	1¹/₂	cups water
¹/₂	teaspoon ground ginger	¹/₃	cup dry white bread crumbs
¹/₈	teaspoon ground cloves	3	tablespoons clarified butter
¹/₂	teaspoon freshly ground pepper	¹/₂	cup heavy cream
¹/₂	teaspoon salt	2	tablespoons all-purpose flour
12	large pitted prunes	¹/₂	teaspoon salt
		2	twists freshly ground pepper

Season the pork with the ginger, cloves, ¹/₂ teaspoon pepper and ¹/₂ teaspoon salt. Simmer the prunes in the water in a saucepan, covered, over medium heat for 20 minutes. Remove from the heat and let stand for 15 minutes. Preheat the oven to 350 degrees. Remove the prunes to a bowl using a slotted spoon, reserving the liquid. Combine the bread crumbs with the prunes. Arrange the prune mixture lengthwise in the center of the pork and roll to enclose the filling. Tie the meat at 1-inch intervals with kitchen twine. Brown the roast on all sides in the butter in an ovenproof skillet over high heat. Add 1 cup of the reserved prune liquid and bring to a boil. Bake, uncovered, for 1¹/₂ hours, basting twice.

Place the pork on a heated platter, remove the twine and tent with foil. Skim the fat from the pan juices. Add the remaining prune liquid to the pan juices and bring to a boil. Whisk in the cream and flour and simmer for 3 minutes. Add ¹/₂ teaspoon salt and 2 twists of pepper. Spoon a little of the sauce over the pork. Slice the pork and serve hot or warm with the warm sauce.

Serves 6 to 8

OF TIDE AND THYME
The Junior League of Annapolis

Cumin Pork Roast with Wild Mushroom Sauce

PORK

1 (3½-pound) center-cut pork loin
   Salt and pepper to taste
1 tablespoon ground cumin

WILD MUSHROOM SAUCE

2 tablespoons butter
8 ounces button mushrooms, sliced
4 ounces each oyster mushrooms and
   shiitake mushrooms, sliced
½ cup chopped shallots
1 garlic clove, minced

1 tablespoons minced jalapeño
   with seeds
2 tablespoons each finely chopped
   fresh cilantro and oregano
1 teaspoon ground cumin
   Salt and pepper to taste
2 tablespoons flour
¼ cup pineapple juice
1 (14-ounce) can chicken broth
1 tablespoon butter
1 teaspoon minced jalapeño with seeds

For the pork, preheat the oven to 375 degrees. Sprinkle the loin with salt and pepper and rub with the cumin. Place in a roasting pan and insert a meat thermometer. Roast for 50 minutes or to 150 degrees on the meat thermometer. Remove to a serving platter and tent with foil.

For the sauce, melt 2 tablespoons butter in a medium skillet over medium heat. Add the mushrooms, shallots, garlic and 1 tablespoon jalapeño. Sauté for 15 minutes or until the mushrooms are very tender and begin to brown. Remove from the heat and add the cilantro, oregano, cumin, salt and pepper. Whisk the flour into the pineapple juice in a medium bowl. Add the chicken broth to the roasting pan, stirring to deglaze. Whisk in the pineapple juice mixture, 1 tablespoon butter and 1 teaspoon jalapeño. Bring to a boil and cook until smooth, whisking constantly. Stir in the mushroom mixture and any accumulated juices from the serving platter. Cook for 5 minutes or until thickened to the desired consistency, stirring occasionally. Adjust the seasonings.

To serve, slice the pork and serve with the sauce. Garnish with fresh cilantro.

Serves 8

ALWAYS IN SEASON
The Junior League of Salt Lake City

The Butcher's Ham Loaf

BROWN SUGAR GLAZE
1/2 cup ketchup
3 tablespoons brown sugar
2 teaspoons prepared mustard

HAM LOAF
1 1/4 pounds ground pork
3/4 pound ground smoked ham
1/4 pound ground beef
1 cup cracker crumbs

1 (8-ounce) can tomato sauce
1 egg
1/2 cup finely chopped onion (optional)

HORSERADISH CREAM
1 cup whipping cream
1/3 cup prepared horseradish
1 teaspoon salt

For the glaze, combine the ketchup and brown sugar in a bowl and mix well. Stir in the mustard.

For the ham loaf, preheat the oven to 350 degrees. Combine the pork, ham, beef, cracker crumbs, tomato sauce, egg and onion in a bowl and mix well. Shape into a loaf and place in a shallow baking pan. Bake for 40 minutes. Top with the glaze. Bake for 30 minutes or until cooked through. Let stand for 10 minutes.

For the horseradish cream, whip the whipping cream in a chilled mixing bowl with chilled beaters until stiff peaks form. Stir in the horseradish and salt. Serve with the ham loaf.

Serves 8

PICNICS, POTLUCKS & PRIZEWINNERS
Indiana 4-H Foundation

The proportions of meat in the ham loaf were created by the butcher in a local grocery store in southern Indiana. The ham loaf was a favorite of his sons who have passed the recipe to mothers-in-law, aunts, and other relatives . . . with requests for its presence on holiday tables in several Indiana and Kentucky homes! Garnish the platter with sage leaves, twists of fresh orange peel, and clusters of currants or grapes.

The Greenbrier's Peppered Maple Turkey Breast

MAPLE SYRUP GLAZE
1   cup West Virginia maple syrup
3   tablespoons light brown sugar
1 1/2 tablespoons Dijon mustard

TURKEY
3   tablespoons cracked black peppercorns
1   tablespoon kosher salt
1   (3- to 3 1/2-pound) boneless skinless turkey breast
1/2 cup (1 stick) butter, cut into 8 slices

For the glaze, combine the maple syrup, brown sugar and Dijon mustard in a small saucepan. Cook until the brown sugar dissolves, stirring constantly to blend well.

For the turkey, preheat the oven to 325 degrees. Mix the peppercorns with the kosher salt in shallow dish. Roll the turkey in the seasoning mixture, coating well. Place on a rack in a roasting pan; insert a meat thermometer into the thickest portion. Roast for 15 minutes; brush with the glaze. Roast for 5 minutes. Top with 4 slices of the butter. Roast for 15 minutes and brush again with the glaze. Roast for 5 minutes.

Place the remaining 4 slices butter on the turkey and roast for 15 minutes longer or to 150 degrees on the meat thermometer. Remove from the oven and brush again with the glaze; the turkey will continue to cook and should reach 160 degrees on the meat thermometer. Let stand for 15 minutes before carving into slices. Overlap the slices on a serving plate.

Combine the pan drippings with the remaining glaze in a small saucepan. Cook over high heat for 3 to 5 minutes or until slightly reduced. Spoon over the turkey slices. Serve warm or at room temperature.

Serves 6 to 8

OH MY STARS!
The Junior League of Roanoke

Cornish Game Hens with Blackberry Honey

4   Cornish game hens
     Salt and pepper to taste
2   cups water
1   cup honey
1/2 cup blackberry jam
1/8 teaspoon cinnamon

Preheat the oven to 450 degrees. Rinse the hens and pat dry. Sprinkle the hens inside and out with salt and pepper. Place in a baking pan. Pour the water around the hens. Bake for 10 minutes.

Combine the honey, jam and cinnamon in a microwave-safe dish and mix well. Microwave for 1 minute or until the jam melts and stir. Brush the hens with the blackberry honey.

Lower the oven temperature to 350 degrees. Bake for 40 minutes longer or until the hens are cooked through, basting with the blackberry honey every 15 minutes.

Serves 4

SOUTHERN ON OCCASION
The Junior League of Cobb-Marietta

Tennessee River Duck and Dressing

CORN BREAD

2 tablespoons melted bacon drippings
2 cups cornmeal
1 1/2 teaspoons salt
1 teaspoon baking soda
2 cups buttermilk
2 eggs

DUCKS

4 ducks, dressed
2 cups chopped onions
2 cups chopped celery
1/2 can Cavender's Greek seasoning
2 teaspoons sage
Salt and pepper to taste
2 (14-ounce) cans chicken broth

For the corn bread, heat the bacon drippings in a cast-iron skillet in a 450-degree oven until smoking. Combine the cornmeal, salt and baking soda in a bowl and mix well. Add the buttermilk and eggs and mix well. Spoon the batter into the hot skillet. Bake for 15 to 20 minutes or until brown. Cool slightly and crumble the corn bread into a large bowl.

For the ducks, combine the ducks with enough water to cover in a stockpot. Boil until the ducks are tender; drain. Let stand until cool. Preheat the oven to 350 degrees. Chop the duck, discarding the skin and bones. Add the duck, onions, celery, Greek seasoning, sage, salt and pepper to the corn bread and toss to mix. Add the broth and mix well. Spoon the duck mixture into a 3-quart baking dish. Bake for 1 1/2 hours or until light brown.

Serves 10 to 12

PROVISIONS & POLITICS
James K. Polk Memorial Association

Seafood Gumbo

5	pounds peeled shrimp	2	links kielbasa sausage
	Salt, black pepper and cayenne pepper to taste	2	(15-ounce) cans tomatoes, chopped
1¹⁄₂	cups vegetable oil	³⁄₄	to 1 (10-ounce) can tomatoes with green chiles
3	cups flour	1	(15-ounce) can tomato sauce
4	large onions, chopped		Worcestershire sauce to taste
3	large bell peppers, chopped	1	(10-ounce) package frozen okra
¹⁄₂	stalk celery, chopped	2	pints oysters
6	to 8 garlic cloves, chopped	1	pound lump crab meat

Boil the shrimp in enough water to cover seasoned with salt, black pepper and cayenne pepper in a stockpot for 5 minutes. Turn off the heat and let stand, covered, for 5 minutes. Drain the shrimp, reserving the liquid. Combine the vegetable oil and flour in a cast-iron skillet. Cook over medium-low heat until the roux is dark brown, stirring constantly to prevent scorching. Sauté the onions, bell peppers, celery and garlic in a small amount of vegetable oil or nonstick cooking spray in a skillet until wilted. Boil the sausage in water to cover in a saucepan to remove some of the fat; drain and discard the liquid. Cut the sausage into ¹⁄₄-inch slices.

Combine the roux, sautéed vegetables, reserved shrimp liquid, tomatoes, tomatoes with green chiles and tomato sauce in a large stockpot and mix well. Add salt, black pepper and Worcestershire sauce. Bring to a simmer, stirring frequently. Add the okra, sausage, shrimp, oysters and crab meat. Simmer for several hours. Serve with filé (an optional condiment) over cooked medium grain rice.

Serves 25 to 30

SETTINGS ON THE DOCK OF THE BAY
ASSISTANCE LEAGUE® of the Bay Area

It often takes up to 45 minutes to create a good roux, but if it ever burns in the process, it should be discarded as it will ruin the flavor of the gumbo. The secret of a good roux is to have the oil very, very hot before adding the flour.

After-Ski Minestrone

4	ounces prosciutto, chopped
1	medium onion, chopped
2	tablespoons olive oil
4	cloves of garlic, chopped
1/2	cup chopped celery
1/2	cup grated carrot
1	cup (medium pieces) fresh green beans
2	cups canned peeled tomatoes
9	cups chicken broth
1/2	teaspoon oregano
1	cup mashed cooked lima beans or cannellini beans
1/2	cup uncooked orzo
1	rosemary sprig
1/2	cup grated Parmesan cheese
	Salt and pepper to taste

Sauté the prosciutto and onion in the heated olive oil in a large saucepan until the onion is tender. Add the garlic and sauté for 1 minute. Add the celery, carrot and green beans. Sauté for 3 minutes.

Add the tomatoes, chicken broth and oregano. Bring to a boil and reduce the heat. Simmer, covered, for 20 minutes or until the vegetables are tender.

Stir in the lima beans, orzo and rosemary. Cook for 15 minutes longer. Discard the rosemary. Add the Parmesan cheese and season with salt and pepper.

Serves 5 to 6

ALWAYS IN SEASON
The Junior League of Salt Lake City

Cajun Green Beans

1   (36-ounce) package frozen cut green beans
2   tablespoons Creole seasoning
1/4   teaspoon red pepper flakes
1/4   cup (or more) chopped red bell pepper
1/2   cup chopped peppered bacon
1/4   cup (or more) chopped onion
1/4   cup chopped celery
2   tablespoons chopped green bell pepper
3/4   cup (1 1/2 sticks) butter

Preheat the oven to 375 degrees. Place the green beans in a large baking dish. Sprinkle with Creole seasoning, red pepper flakes, red pepper, bacon, onion, celery and green pepper. Dot with the butter. Bake for 30 minutes or until the green beans are tender and bright green in color, stirring every 10 minutes. This may be prepared ahead and frozen until ready to bake.

Serves 14 to 16

SETTINGS ON THE DOCK OF THE BAY
ASSISTANCE LEAGUE® of the Bay Area

Carrot and Sweet Potato Purée

4   large sweet potatoes (about 2 pounds)
1   pound carrots
1   tablespoon sugar (optional)
1/2   cup (1 stick) butter, softened
     Salt and pepper to taste
1/2   cup sour cream
1/2   teaspoon grated nutmeg

Preheat the oven to 400 degrees. Scrub the potatoes and cut slits in the tops. Place in an 8×10-inch baking pan. Bake for 1 hour and 15 minutes or until tender. Let stand until cool enough to handle. Cut the carrots into 1-inch pieces. Place in a saucepan and cover with water. Add the sugar. Bring to a boil and cook, covered, for 30 minutes or until tender. Drain the carrots and add the butter, salt and pepper. Place the carrot mixture and the sweet potato pulp in a food processor. Add the sour cream and process until smooth. Add the nutmeg and more salt and pepper if necessary. Pour into an ovenproof dish. Refrigerate if not serving immediately. To reheat, bake, covered, at 350 degrees for 25 minutes or until hot.

Serves 8

STEAMBOAT SEASONS
Guild of Strings in the Mountains
Music Festival

Surprise Corn Pudding

2	(15-ounce) cans whole kernel corn, drained
1/4	cup flour
1	tablespoon cornmeal
3	tablespoons sugar
3	tablespoons butter or margarine, melted
3/4	cup milk
2	eggs
1/8	teaspoon cinnamon
1/8	teaspoon nutmeg
1/4	teaspoon vanilla extract (optional)

Preheat the oven to 350 degrees. Process 1 can of corn in a blender until smooth, scraping down the sides. Combine with the remaining can of corn, flour, cornmeal, sugar and butter in a bowl and mix well. Whisk the milk, eggs, cinnamon, nutmeg and vanilla in a separate bowl. Stir into the corn mixture. Spoon into a greased shallow 2-quart baking dish. Bake for 35 minutes or until set.

Serves 8

FROM BLACK TIE TO BLACKEYED PEAS
Dr. Victor Irving

Leeks in Saffron Cream Sauce

3	large leeks, trimmed
1/4	cup heavy cream
1	pinch of saffron threads
1/2	cup heavy cream
1/2	cup freshly grated Parmesan cheese
	Salt to taste

Cut the leeks in half lengthwise. Open the leaves and rinse thoroughly under cold water. Cook the leeks in boiling water in a large saucepan until tender crisp at the root ends; drain. Cut the leeks in half and return to the pan. Heat 1/4 cup heavy cream in a small saucepan over very low heat. Stir in the saffron threads and let stand for 5 minutes. Stir in 1/2 cup heavy cream and the cheese. Heat the sauce and add the salt. Spoon over the leeks. Simmer, uncovered, for 5 minutes or until the leeks are tender.

Serves 6

TASTES, TALES AND TRADITIONS
Palo Alto Auxiliary

Company Peas

6   tablespoons butter
2/3 cup chopped onion
3   cups thinly sliced celery
3   or 4 (10-ounce) packages frozen
    green peas
1/4 cup (or more) hot water
11/2 teaspoons salt
    Pepper to taste
    Thyme to taste
1   teaspoon Worcestershire sauce
2   tablespoons chopped fresh parsley

Melt the butter in a sauté pan. Add the onion and celery. Sauté for 5 minutes or until golden brown. Add the peas, hot water, salt, pepper and thyme. Simmer, covered, for 8 minutes or until the peas are tender. Do not overcook. Add the Worcestershire sauce and parsley and mix lightly.

Serves 8 to 10

SEABOARD TO SIDEBOARD
The Junior League of Wilmington

Creamy Mashed Potatoes

8   to 10 potatoes, peeled and chopped
    Salt to taste
1/2 cup (1 stick) butter, softened
1/4 cup milk
1   cup sour cream
8   ounces cream cheese, softened
1   teaspoon garlic salt
1   teaspoon salt
3   to 4 tablespoons butter
    Paprika to taste

Cook the potatoes in salted water to cover in a saucepan until tender; drain. Add 1/2 cup butter and the milk and mash until smooth. Beat in the sour cream, cream cheese, garlic salt and 1 teaspoon salt until smooth. Spoon into a greased 9×13-inch baking dish. Chill, covered, in the refrigerator for 24 hours. Remove from the refrigerator and let stand at room temperature for 2 to 3 hours. Preheat the oven to 350 degrees. Top with 3 to 4 tablespoons butter. Sprinkle with paprika. Bake for 30 minutes.

Serves 8

HOME AGAIN, HOME AGAIN
The Junior League of Owensboro

Garlic Mashed Potatoes

8   medium russet potatoes, peeled and
      cut into pieces
8   cloves of garlic, peeled and
      thinly sliced
5   tablespoons butter or margarine
1   teaspoon salt
      Milk
3/4 cup grated Parmesan cheese

Cook the potatoes and garlic in boiling
salted water in a saucepan for 20 to
25 minutes or until very tender; drain.
Mash with the butter and salt, adding
enough milk to make of the desired
consistency. Blend in the cheese. Whip
with and electric mixer until fluffy.
Garnish with fresh rosemary sprigs.
Serve immediately.

Serves 8

BEYOND BURLAP
The Junior League of Boise

The Official Miss Forbus' Squash Casserole

8   yellow squash, sliced
1   cup chopped onion
1/2 teaspoon salt
      Dash of pepper
1   tablespoon margarine
1   cup bread crumbs
3   eggs, beaten
3/4 cup milk
1   cup (4 ounces) shredded cheese

Combine the squash, onion, salt, pepper,
margarine and a small amount of water
in a saucepan. Cook until the squash in
tender; drain well. Preheat the oven to
350 degrees. Mix the cooked squash,
bread crumbs, eggs and milk in a bowl.
Spoon into a baking dish. Bake for
25 minutes. Top with the cheese and
bake for 5 to 6 minutes longer or until
the cheese melts.

Serves 6 to 8

SOUTHERN GRACE
Mississippi University for Women

Spinach Madeleine

2	(10-ounce) packages frozen chopped spinach
1/4	cup (1/2 stick) butter
2	tablespoons flour
2	tablespoons chopped onion
2	teaspoons finely chopped fresh jalapeño peppers
6	ounces Velveeta cheese, chopped
1/2	cup evaporated milk
1	teaspoon Worcestershire sauce
3/4	teaspoon celery salt
3/4	teaspoon garlic salt
	Salt to taste
1/2	teaspoon black pepper
	Red pepper to taste

Cook the spinach using the package directions; drain, reserving the liquid. Melt the butter in a saucepan over low heat. Add the flour and stir until blended and smooth. Do not brown. Add the onion and cook until softened but not brown. Add the reserved liquid slowly, stirring constantly to avoid lumps forming. Cook until smooth and thickened, stirring constantly. Add the jalapeño peppers, cheese, evaporated milk, Worcestershire sauce, celery salt, garlic salt, salt, black pepper and red pepper and stir until the cheese is melted. Combine with the spinach and mix well. Serve immediately or put into a baking dish and top with buttered bread crumbs. The flavor is improved if the latter is done and the dish is refrigerated overnight. Bake until heated through. This may also be frozen.

Serves 5 to 6

RIVER ROAD RECIPES
The Junior League of Baton Rouge

Praline Sweet Potatoes

POTATOES
1 (29-ounce) can sweet potatoes
3 tablespoons butter
1/4 cup packed brown sugar
1/4 teaspoon salt
   Whipping cream

TOPPING
2/3 cup packed brown sugar
1 tablespoon whipping cream
1/2 cup chopped pecans
3 tablespoons butter
1/2 teaspoon ground cinnamon
1/4 teaspoon ground nutmeg
1/8 teaspoon salt
1/4 teaspoon ground ginger
1/8 teaspoon ground cloves

For the potatoes, heat the undrained sweet potatoes in a saucepan until heated through; drain. Combine with the butter, brown sugar and salt in a bowl. Mash well, adding enough whipping cream to make of the desired consistency. Spoon into a buttered 2-quart baking dish. Preheat the oven to 350 degrees.

For the topping, combine the brown sugar, whipping cream, pecans, butter, cinnamon, nutmeg, salt, ginger and cloves in a small saucepan. Cook over medium heat until the butter is melted, stirring until smooth. Spread over the sweet potatoes.

Bake for 10 to 15 minutes or until bubbly.

Serves 6 to 8

BEYOND BURLAP
The Junior League of Boise

An alternative way to prepare this dish is to cut the sweet potatoes into 1/4-inch slices and arrange in a buttered baking dish. Spread the topping over the slices and bake for 10 to 15 minutes or until bubbly. This dish can be prepared and refrigerated for up to 2 days before baking.

Fresh Cranberry Apple Relish

1   pound fresh cranberries
1   orange, unpeeled, seeded
1   apple, unpeeled, cored and seeded
3/4   cup sugar
1/2   cup chopped walnuts

Combine 1/2 the cranberries, 1/2 the unpeeled orange, 1/2 the unpeeled apple and 1/2 the sugar in a food processor container. Process for 30 to 45 seconds. Remove to a bowl. Repeat with the remaining cranberries, orange, apple and sugar. Stir in the walnuts. Cover and chill for at least 1 hour before serving.

Serves 8

FROM THE COAST TO THE CASCADES
The Junior League of Eugene

Baked Pineapple

1   (20-ounce) can pineapple chunks
3/4   cup sugar
3   tablespoons flour
1   cup (4 ounces) shredded mild
      Cheddar cheese
11/2   cups crushed butter crackers
1/4   cup (1/2 stick) butter, melted

Preheat the oven to 350 degrees. Drain the pineapple, reserving 3 tablespoons pineapple syrup. Mix the sugar, flour and pineapple syrup in a saucepan over low heat, stirring until the sugar dissolves. Remove from the heat. Add the pineapple and cheese. Spoon the pineapple mixture into an 8×8-inch baking dish. Sprinkle the crackers over the pineapple. Drizzle the butter over the crackers. Bake for 20 to 25 minutes.

Serves 6

BEYOND THE RIM
The Junior League of Amarillo

Corn Bread Dressing

4 cups chicken broth
1 1/2 cups chopped onions
4 cups crumbled corn bread
6 cups torn bread pieces
6 eggs, beaten

Preheat the oven to 400 degrees. Combine the broth and onions in a saucepan over medium heat. Cook for 15 minutes. Combine with the corn bread, bread pieces and eggs in a bowl and mix well. Spoon into a 9×13-inch baking dish. Bake for 35 minutes.

Serves 8

TAKE FIVE, A HOLIDAY COOKBOOK
Debbye Dabbs

Turkey Dressing

Turkey giblets and neck
2 teaspoons salt
1 large onion, finely chopped
6 cups seasoned bread crumbs or bread cubes
1 cup warm water
1/3 cup butter
6 medium potatoes, peeled boiled and crushed into chunks
Salt to taste

Combine the giblets, neck, 2 teaspoons salt and water to cover in a saucepan. Boil for 25 minutes. Drain, reserving the cooking liquid. Let the meat cool slightly. Remove the meat from the neck. Process the neck meat, giblets and onion in a meat grinder or food processor. Preheat the oven to 325 degrees.

Combine the bread crumbs and warm water in a medium bowl. If using bread cubes, stir until crumbly. Combine the butter, reserved cooking liquid, meat mixture, bread crumbs and potatoes in a large bowl. Add additional water if needed. Season with salt. Spoon the dressing into a greased baking pan. Bake for 45 to 55 minutes.

Serves 10 to 12

BEYOND BURLAP
The Junior League of Boise

Savannah River Red Rice

1 cup tomato juice
1¹/₂ cups chicken broth
2 tablespoons tomato paste
¹/₈ teaspoon cayenne
¹/₂ teaspoon salt
¹/₄ teaspoon white pepper
¹/₂ cup chopped onion
¹/₂ cup finely chopped celery
¹/₄ cup chopped green bell pepper
6 tablespoons olive oil
2 cups parboiled rice

Combine the juice, broth, tomato paste, cayenne, salt and white pepper in a large ovenproof saucepan. Bring to a simmer. Sauté the onion, celery and green pepper in the oil in a skillet until tender. Stir in the rice, coating with oil. Add the rice mixture to the tomato mixture and mix well. Bring to a boil. Bake, covered, at 350 degrees or simmer for 20 to 25 minutes. For variation, you may add 4 ounces hot cooked sausage before baking.

Serves 6

FROM BLACK TIE TO BLACKEYED PEAS
Dr. Victor Irving

Foolproof Homemade Yeast Rolls

1 cup shortening
1 cup sugar
1 tablespoon salt
1 cup boiling water
2 envelopes dry yeast
1 cup warm water
4 eggs, beaten
6 cups all-purpose flour

Combine the shortening, sugar and salt in a bowl. Add the boiling water and stir until the shortening melts. Let cool to lukewarm. Dissolve the yeast in the warm water in a bowl and let stand for 5 minutes or until the yeast slightly foams. Add the dissolved yeast and eggs to the shortening mixture and mix well. Stir in the flour, 1 cup at a time, to make a stiff dough. Cover and chill for 12 hours. Remove from the refrigerator 3 hours before baking. Knead the dough a few times on a well-floured work surface. Roll out the dough and cut with a 2-inch biscuit cutter. Arrange the rolls in a greased baking pan. Let rise in a warm place for 3 hours. Preheat the oven to 400 degrees. Bake for 12 to 15 minutes or until golden brown.

Makes 2 dozen rolls

PAR 3 TEA TIME AT THE MASTERS®
The Junior League of Augusta

Desserts

Several years ago, my aunt began hosting the traditional gathering of her husband's family on Christmas night. This was something her mother-in-law had always done, but her health was declining, so my aunt, who loves to entertain, was happy to keep the tradition going. Included in the group of more than thirty people were her husband's children and grandchildren, brothers and their families, as well as my aunt's two daughters, my husband, and me. What a ruckus we created, with everyone talking at once, the children playing tag, and laughter carrying throughout the house.

My aunt and her husband set tables up all through the house and decorated them with festive centerpieces of greenery, ribbons, and candles. They brought out the good china, silverware, and silver water goblets, which, after having been painstakingly polished earlier in the day by my cousins, glistened against the candlelight. That first year we feasted on a huge traditional Christmas dinner of turkey, dressing, and all the trimmings. Afterward, we had our choice of pies, cakes, cookies, and candies, along with my uncle's "famous" warm mulled cider. We exchanged gifts, sang carols, and everyone went home with full bellies and full hearts.

The family has grown, and my aunt and her husband have slowed a bit. So in order to make the preparation easier, there have been several variations to that first holiday dinner. One year we had ham, another year barbecue, and one year we tried an hors d'oeuvre and dessert buffet. We have even had homemade lasagna, not exactly traditional Christmas fare. Packed away are the good china and silverware, replaced after that first year with everyday flatware and plastic plates.

In order to accommodate so many busy schedules and folks coming from out of town, the date of our gathering was changed, and now we get together before Christmas. No matter what the date is or what is on the menu, we cherish the time we get to spend together and look forward to it all year long. And there are some things that have remained the same through the years: we still drink from just-polished silver water goblets, and we still go home with full bellies and full hearts.

TANIS WESTBROOK

Sugarplum Dessert Party

What the Dickens? Bread Pudding

BREAD PUDDING
1¹/₂ cups sugar
3 eggs, lightly beaten
2 tablespoons light brown sugar
¹/₂ teaspoon nutmeg
2³/₄ cups whipping cream
¹/₄ cup (¹/₂ stick) melted butter
4 cups French bread cubes
³/₄ cup raisins

VANILLA SAUCE
1¹/₄ cups whipping cream
¹/₂ cup sugar
3 tablespoons light brown sugar
2 tablespoons butter
1 tablespoon flour
1 egg
¹/₈ teaspoon nutmeg
1 tablespoon vanilla extract

To prepare the pudding, preheat the oven to 375 degrees. Mix the sugar, eggs, brown sugar and nutmeg in a bowl. Stir in the whipping cream and butter. Fold in the bread cubes and raisins. Spoon into a lightly greased 2-quart soufflé dish or deep baking dish. Bake for 30 minutes; cover loosely with foil. Cook for 20 to 25 minutes longer. Let stand for 10 minutes before serving.

To prepare the sauce, whisk the whipping cream, sugar, brown sugar, butter, flour, egg and nutmeg in a saucepan. Cook for 10 to 12 minutes or until thickened, whisking constantly. Remove from the heat. Stir in the vanilla. Serve warm or at room temperature with the bread pudding.

Serves 6 to 8

SOUTHERN ON OCCASION
The Junior League of Cobb-Marietta

A Holiday Memory From Dierbergs

For almost thirty years, Dierbergs has been creating delicious recipes for our customers to enjoy. Whether it's for a special occasion or a quick weeknight meal, they can count on our recipes to be accurate, reliable, and, of course, to taste great. So it is quite a compliment when one of our holiday desserts took St. Louis by storm.

In 1993, we introduced our recipe for White Chocolate Mousse Torte at the start of the holiday season. The impressive yet simple-to-make dessert features a rich, creamy filling surrounded by crisp rolled pirouette cookies. One by one, boxes of the cookies disappeared from our store shelves. Despite many frantic phone calls to replenish the stock, our suppliers had no more cookies to send. Even our competitors sold out! The dessert was so popular that one of our associates returned the two boxes she purchased for herself so that customers could buy them. We knew we had a hit when the cookie manufacturer called us and requested that we give them advance notice if we decided to promote the recipe again!

White Chocolate Mousse Torte

1   can (14.1 ounces) chocolate-filled pirouette cookies
3   cups (18 ounces) white baking chips
2   packages (8 ounces each) cream cheese, softened
1   teaspoon almond extract
2   tablespoons honey
2   cups heavy whipping cream, whipped
     Grated semi-sweet chocolate (optional)

Using a serrated knife, carefully cut the cookies into 3-inch pieces. Stand the cookies around the inside edge of an 8-inch springform pan. Crush the trim pieces and enough remaining cookies to make 1 cup crumbs; spread in the bottom of the pan. Place the white baking chips in a medium microwave-safe bowl. Microwave (high) and stir in 30-second intervals, until the chips are melted. With a hand mixer, beat in the cream cheese, almond extract and honey until smooth. Gently fold in the whipped cream. Carefully pour the mixture into the center of the prepared springform pan; spread and smooth the top. Cover and refrigerate for at least 6 hours before serving. (If desired, freeze the torte for up to 1 month. The filling will have an ice cream-like consistency when served frozen.) If desired, garnish top with grated chocolate.

Serves 16

THE BEST OF DIERBERGS
Dierbergs Markets, Inc.

This impressive no-bake torte is simple to make and heavenly to eat. Adorn the torte with a festive ribbon for presentation. Remove the ribbon just before serving.

Graham Cracker Torte

3 egg whites
1/4 teaspoon cream of tartar
1/2 cup sugar
1/4 cup graham cracker crumbs
1 teaspoon baking powder
1/2 cup sugar
1/2 cup finely chopped almonds
   or pecans
1 teaspoon vanilla extract
1 cup whipping cream, whipped

Preheat the oven to 325 degrees. Beat the egg whites and cream of tartar in a mixing bowl until stiff peaks form. Beat in 1/2 cup sugar gradually. Mix the graham cracker crumbs, baking powder and 1/2 cup sugar in a bowl. Fold into the egg white mixture. Fold in the almonds and vanilla. Spread in a buttered pie plate. Bake for 25 to 30 minutes. Cool on a wire rack. Serve with the whipped cream.

Serves 6

SOUTHERN GRACE
Mississippi University for Women

Cranberry Apple Crisp

2 cups packed brown sugar, divided
1/2 cup cornmeal
1 cup old-fashioned oats
1/2 cup (1 stick) butter, softened
6 large tart green apples, peeled, cored
   and sliced
1 tablespoon lemon juice
2 cups cranberries, fresh or frozen
   (cherries can be substituted)
   Vanilla ice cream or whipped cream

Preheat the oven to 350 degrees. Combine 1 cup brown sugar, the cornmeal and oats in a small bowl. Cut in the butter with a fork or hands until crumbly. Set aside. (It can be made ahead and refrigerated.)

Mix the apples with the lemon juice in a 9×13-inch glass baking dish. Add the cranberries and remaining 1 cup brown sugar. Mix well. Sprinkle with the topping mixture, covering the fruit evenly.

Bake for 55 to 60 minutes or until the apples are tender when pierced with a knife, the juices are bubbly and the top is golden brown. Serve warm with ice cream or whipped cream.

Serves 6 to 8

STEAMBOAT SEASONS
Guild of Strings in the Mountains
Music Festival

Pumpkin Pie Crunch

1	(16-ounce) can solid-pack pumpkin
1	(12-ounce) can evaporated milk
1 1/2	cups sugar
3	eggs, lightly beaten
4	teaspoons pumpkin pie spice
1/2	teaspoon salt
1	(2-layer) package yellow cake mix
1	cup (2 sticks) butter, melted

Preheat the oven to 350 degrees. Grease the bottom of a 9×13-inch baking pan. Combine the pumpkin, evaporated milk, sugar, eggs, pie spice and salt in a bowl and mix well. Spoon the pumpkin mixture into the prepared pan.

Sprinkle the cake mix evenly over the top of the prepared layer and drizzle with the butter. Bake for 50 to 55 minutes or until golden brown. Let stand until cool. Garnish with whipped topping and chopped pecans. Store in the refrigerator.

Serves 15

HOME AGAIN, HOME AGAIN
The Junior League of Owensboro

Cranberry Marsh Ice

1	envelope unflavored gelatin
1	cup cold water
1	(12-ounce) bag cranberries, sorted and rinsed
1 3/4	cups water
2	cups sugar
1/4	cup lemon juice
	Dash of salt

Soften the gelatin in 1 cup cold water in a small bowl. Combine the cranberries, 1 3/4 cups water, the sugar and lemon juice in a large saucepan and bring to a boil. Cook over medium heat for 5 minutes or until the cranberries pop. Pour into a mesh strainer set over a medium bowl and press the cranberries through the strainer using the back of a spoon. Reserve the pulp and liquid and discard the skins. Add the gelatin mixture and salt to the cranberry purée and mix well. Spoon the mixture into a freezer-safe container and freeze, covered, for 8 to 10 hours or until solid. Put the frozen mixture into a blender or food processor and blend until slushy. Refreeze. Serve frozen.

Serves 12

BLACK TIE & BOOTS
University of Wyoming

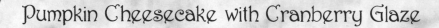

Pumpkin Cheesecake with Cranberry Glaze

GRAHAM CRACKER CRUST
3/4 cup graham cracker crumbs
3 tablespoons butter, melted
2 tablespoons brown sugar
1 teaspoon cinnamon

FILLING
32 ounces cream cheese, softened
1 1/2 cups sugar
5 eggs
1/4 cup flour
1 teaspoon ground cinnamon

1/2 teaspoon ground nutmeg
1/4 teaspoon ground ginger
1/4 teaspoon ground cloves
1 (16-ounce) can pumpkin
1 teaspoon rum extract

CRANBERRY GLAZE
2 cups fresh cranberries
1 cup sugar
1/2 cup water
1 tablespoon cornstarch
1/4 cup sugar

For the crust, mix the graham cracker crumbs, butter, brown sugar and cinnamon in a bowl. Press over the bottom of a 9-inch springform pan.

For the filling, preheat the oven to 325 degrees. Beat the cream cheese in a mixing bowl until smooth. Add the sugar gradually, beating until light and fluffy. Beat in the eggs one at a time. Add a mixture of the flour and spices gradually and mix well. Add the pumpkin gradually, mixing well. Stir in the rum extract. Spoon the filling into the prepared crust. Bake for 1 1/4 hours or just until the center is slightly firm to the touch, checking after 45 minutes; do not overbake. Cool on a wire rack.

For the glaze, combine the cranberries, 1 cup sugar and water in a saucepan. Bring to a boil and cook for 2 minutes. Mix the cornstarch with 1/4 cup sugar and stir into the cranberries. Bring to a boil and cook until thickened, stirring constantly. Cool to room temperature. Spread the glaze over the cheesecake. Chill, covered, in the refrigerator for 8 hours or longer. Place on a serving plate and remove the side of the pan.

Serves 16

FIRST IMPRESSIONS
The Junior League of Waterloo-Cedar Falls

Crème Parisienne with Raspberry Sauce

RASPBERRY SAUCE
1   (10- or 12-ounce) package frozen
     sweetened raspberries, thawed
1/3 cup seedless raspberry preserves
1   tablespoon fresh lemon juice

CRÈME PARISIENNE
1   envelope unflavored gelatin
1/4 cup cold water
12   ounces cream cheese, cut into pieces
1   cup heavy whipping cream
2/3 cup sugar
13/4 cups sour cream
3/4 teaspoon vanilla extract
30   fresh raspberries (optional)

For the sauce, press the raspberries through a sieve into a bowl, discarding the seeds. Add the preserves and lemon juice to the purée and mix well. Chill, covered, until serving time.

For the crème, double-coat ten 4-ounce molds (not Tupperware) with nonstick cooking spray. Soften the gelatin in the water. Heat the cream cheese, cream and sugar in the top of a double boiler over simmering water. Cook until smooth, stirring constantly with a whisk. Stir in the softened gelatin. Cook until the gelatin completely dissolves, stirring constantly. Remove from the heat and stir in the sour cream and vanilla. Pour into the prepared molds. Chill for 4 hours or longer. Let stand at room temperature for 20 to 30 minutes before serving. Dip the molds in hot water for a few seconds to loosen. Run a knife around the side of the mold if necessary. Unmold onto individual dessert plates. Spoon raspberry sauce around each mold. Place 3 raspberries in the sauce around each dessert. Garnish with fresh mint sprigs.

Serves 10

TASTES, TALES AND TRADITIONS
Palo Alto Auxiliary

Christmas Pie

PIE
6   all-purpose apples, peeled and sliced
1   cup fresh cranberries
1   cup chopped dates
1/4   teaspoon ground cinnamon
1/4   teaspoon ground cloves
3   tablespoons all-purpose flour
3/4   to 1 cup sugar
1/2   cup water
1/2   cup chopped walnuts

PASTRY CRUST
1   cup all-purpose flour
1/4   teaspoon salt
1/3   to 1/2 cup shortening
2   tablespoons cold water

For the pie, combine the apples, cranberries, dates, cinnamon and cloves in a large bowl. Add the flour and mix well. Combine the sugar and water in a large saucepan; bring to a boil. Reduce the heat and stir in the apple mixture. Cook for 10 minutes, stirring occasionally. Cool slightly. Stir in the walnuts. Spoon into the prepared crust, spreading evenly. Cool before slicing. Garnish with baked pastry cut into holiday shapes.

For the crust, preheat the oven to 450 degrees. Combine the flour and salt in a small bowl. Cut in the shortening until crumbly. Add the water, 1 tablespoon at a time, mixing with a fork until the mixture forms a ball. Roll into a 10-inch circle on a lightly floured surface. Fit into a 9-inch pie plate. Flute the edge. Line the pastry shell with foil to cover; fill with pie weights or dried beans. Bake for 12 to 15 minutes or until golden brown. Cool.

Serves 8

CELEBRATE COLORADO
Junior Service League of Grand Junction

Pineapple Coconut Chess Pie

1 1/2 cups sugar
3   tablespoons cornmeal
2   tablespoons flour
1/4   teaspoon salt
4   eggs, lightly beaten
1   teaspoon vanilla extract
1/4   cup (1/2 stick) butter, melted
1   (16-ounce) can crushed pineapple, drained
1   (3-ounce) can flaked coconut
1   unbaked (9-inch) pie shell

Preheat the oven to 350 degrees. Mix the sugar, cornmeal, flour and salt in a mixing bowl. Add the eggs and vanilla and mix well. Stir in the butter, pineapple and coconut. Spoon into the pie shell. Bake for 40 minutes. Cover with foil and bake for 20 minutes longer or until set. Cool on a wire rack.

Serves 6 to 8

BEACH APPÉTIT
The Junior League of the Emerald Coast

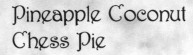 *This pie is so easy to make. Be sure to make several at a time and give to friends or neighbors during the holidays.*

Pecan Pies

2   all ready pie pastries
1   cup (2 sticks) margarine
1 1/4 cups light corn syrup
1   cup sugar
1   cup packed brown sugar
4   eggs, beaten
1   teaspoon lemon juice
2   teaspoons vanilla extract
      Dash of salt
2 1/2 cups chopped pecans

Prepare the pie pastries using the package directions for two 9-inch baked pie crusts. Cook the margarine in a saucepan until golden brown; cool. Preheat the oven to 425 degrees. Combine the corn syrup, sugar, brown sugar, eggs, lemon juice, vanilla and salt in a bowl and mix well. Stir in the pecans. Add the browned margarine and mix well. Spoon into the prepared pie crusts. Bake for 10 minutes. Reduce the temperature to 325 degrees. Bake for 40 minutes, covering the edges with foil if needed.

Serves 12 to 16

FROM BLACK TIE TO BLACKEYED PEAS
Dr. Victor Irving

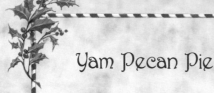

Yam Pecan Pie

TOPPING
1/4 cup (1/2 stick) butter, softened
1/2 cup packed brown sugar
3/4 cup finely chopped pecans

PIE
1 cup mashed cooked or canned sweet potatoes
1/3 cup packed brown sugar
3/4 teaspoon cinnamon
1/8 teaspoon salt
1 (5-ounce) can evaporated milk
2 eggs, beaten
1 unbaked (9-inch) pie shell
Whipped cream (optional)

For the topping, mix the butter, brown sugar and pecans in a bowl until crumbly.

For the pie filling, preheat the oven to 375 degrees. Combine the sweet potatoes, brown sugar, cinnamon, salt, evaporated milk and eggs in a large bowl and mix well. Pour into the pie shell. Bake for 20 minutes. Sprinkle with the topping. Bake for 25 minutes longer. Let cool. Serve with whipped cream.

Serves 6 to 8

BEYOND BURLAP
The Junior League of Boise

If using fresh sweet potatoes, add 1/3 cup sugar to the sweet potatoes. Cool slightly before mixing with the other ingredients.

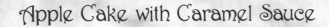
Apple Cake with Caramel Sauce

CAKE

2	eggs
4	cups finely chopped peeled apples
2	cups sugar
2	teaspoons cinnamon
1/2	cup vegetable oil
2	cups flour
2	teaspoons baking soda
1	teaspoon salt

CARAMEL SAUCE

1/2	cup (1 stick) butter
1/2	cup sugar
1/2	cup packed brown sugar
1/2	teaspoon vanilla extract
1/2	cup half-and-half

For the cake, preheat the oven to 350 degrees. Beat the eggs in a large mixing bowl. Add the apples and mix well. Stir in the sugar. Add the cinnamon, oil, flour, baking soda and salt and mix well. The batter will be thick. Pour into a greased 9×13-inch cake pan. Bake for 45 minutes.

For the sauce, melt the butter in a saucepan. Stir in the sugar, brown sugar, vanilla and half-and-half. Bring to a boil to dissolve the sugar, stirring occasionally. Serve warm over the cake.

Serves 12 to 16

DINING DAKOTA STYLE
The Junior League of Sioux Falls

Hummingbird Cake

CAKE

3   cups flour
2   cups sugar
1   teaspoon salt
1   teaspoon baking soda
1   teaspoon cinnamon
3   eggs, beaten
1 1/2   cups vegetable oil
1 1/2   teaspoons vanilla extract
1   (8-ounce) can crushed pineapple,
    drained
1   cup chopped pecans or walnuts
2   cups chopped bananas, mashed

CREAM CHEESE FROSTING

16   ounces cream cheese, softened
1   cup (2 sticks) margarine, softened
2   (1-pound) packages confectioners'
    sugar
2   teaspoons vanilla extract
Chopped pecans (optional)

For the cake, preheat the oven to 350 degrees. Combine the flour, sugar, salt, baking soda and cinnamon in a large bowl and mix well. Add the eggs and oil and stir until moistened; do not beat. Stir in the vanilla, pineapple, 1 cup pecans and bananas; do not beat. Spoon into 3 greased and floured 9-inch cake pans. Bake for 25 to 30 minutes or until the cake tests done. Cool in the pans for 10 minutes. Remove to wire racks to cool completely.

For the frosting, beat the cream cheese and margarine in a mixing bowl until well blended. Add the confectioners' sugar and beat until light and fluffy. Add the vanilla and beat until of spreading consistency. Spread between the layers and over the top and side of the cooled cake. Sprinkle with chopped pecans if desired.

Serves 12

MARVELOUS MORSELS
Maggie Ruth Smith

Mochaccino Cake

1	(2-layer) package devil's food cake mix
3	eggs
1	cup water
1/2	cup heavy whipping cream
1/4	cup vegetable oil
2	tablespoons baking cocoa
2	tablespoons instant coffee powder
1	cup miniature chocolate chips
2	tablespoons heavy whipping cream
2	tablespoons instant coffee powder
2	(16-ounce) containers vanilla frosting

Preheat the oven to 350 degrees. Combine the cake mix, eggs, water, 1/2 cup heavy cream, oil, baking cocoa and 2 tablespoons coffee powder in a bowl. Beat with an electric mixer at low speed until blended. Beat at medium speed for 2 minutes. Stir in the chocolate chips. Pour into 2 greased and floured 9-inch cake pans.

Bake for 25 to 30 minutes or until a wooden pick inserted in the center comes out clean. Cool in the pans for 20 minutes. Remove to a wire rack to cool completely.

Mix 2 tablespoons heavy cream and 2 tablespoons coffee powder in a bowl. Add the vanilla frosting and stir to mix well. Spread between the layers and over the top and side of the cake.

Serves 12

PAR 3 TEA TIME AT THE MASTERS®
The Junior League of Augusta

Pound Cake

3   cups flour
3   cups sugar
1   cup (2 sticks) butter
6   eggs
1   cup heavy cream
1/2 teaspoon almond extract
1/2 teaspoon vanilla extract
    Zesty Lemon Sauce

Sift the flour twice. Beat the sugar and butter in a mixing bowl until creamy, scraping the bowl occasionally. Add the eggs 1 at a time, beating for 1 minute after each addition. Add the flour alternately with the heavy cream, beginning and ending with the flour and beating well after each addition. Stir in the flavorings. Spoon the batter into a buttered and floured tube pan. Place the pan in a cold oven. Bake at 300 degrees for 1 1/2 hours. Cool in the pan for 10 minutes. Remove to a wire rack to cool completely. Serve with the Zesty Lemon Sauce.

Serves 16

Provisions & Politics
James K. Polk Memorial Association

Zesty Lemon Sauce

2/3 cup sugar
    Zest of 1 lemon
5   egg yolks
1/2 cup lemon juice
1/8 teaspoon salt
1/2 cup (1 stick) butter

Process the sugar and lemon zest in a food processor until the lemon zest is minced. Add the egg yolks, lemon juice and salt. Process until mixed. Heat the butter in a saucepan until melted. Add the hot butter to the lemon mixture, processing constantly until blended. Pour the lemon mixture into a saucepan. Cook over low heat until thickened, stirring constantly; do not boil. Store, covered, in the refrigerator. Serve over pound cake or spoon into tart shells.

Makes about 2 cups

Provisions & Politics
James K. Polk Memorial Association

Fondant Cookies with Fondant Icing

COOKIES

1/2	cup (1 stick) butter or margarine, softened
1	cup sugar
1	egg
2	envelopes premelted unsweetened chocolate, or 2 ounces unsweetened chocolate, melted
1/3	cup milk
1	teaspoon vanilla extract
2	cups flour
1	cup chopped pecans (optional)
1/2	teaspoon baking powder
1/2	teaspoon salt

ICING

2	cups confectioners' sugar
2	tablespoons light corn syrup
2	tablespoons (about) hot water
1	teaspoon almond extract
	Red food coloring
1/4	teaspoon peppermint extract
	Green food coloring

For the cookies, beat the butter, sugar, egg, chocolate, milk and vanilla in a large mixing bowl. Mix in the flour, pecans, baking powder and salt at low speed until a soft dough forms, scraping down the side of the bowl constantly. Chill, covered, for 1 to 2 hours or until firm enough to handle. Preheat the oven to 400 degrees. Shape the dough by rounded teaspoonfuls into balls. Place 2 inches apart on an ungreased cookie sheet. Bake for about 7 minutes. Cool on a wire rack.

For the icing, combine the confectioners' sugar, corn syrup and water in a small bowl. (If the icing is too thin, add more confectioners' sugar to thicken.) Pour half the icing into another bowl. Stir the almond extract and a desired amount of red food coloring into half the icing. Stir the peppermint extract and a desired amount of green food coloring into the other half. Swirl the tops of the cookies into either the red or the green icing.

Makes about 4 dozen cookies

ONCE UPON A TIME
The Junior League of Evansville

Quickie Bars

    Graham crackers
1   cup chopped nuts
1   cup packed brown sugar
1   cup (2 sticks) butter
8   (6-ounce) milk chocolate bars

Preheat the oven to 400 degrees. Line a 10×15-inch baking pan with graham crackers. Sprinkle with the nuts. Combine the brown sugar and butter in a saucepan. Bring to a boil. Boil for 2 minutes or until blended, stirring frequently. Pour over the chopped nuts. Bake for 6 to 8 minutes. Remove from the oven. Layer the chocolate bars over the top. Let stand until the chocolate is softened. Spread the softened chocolate over the top. Cut into bars immediately.

Serves 50

THE BOUNTY OF CHESTER COUNTY
Chester County Agricultural
Development Council

Snow-Capped Hot Chocolate

1   cup semisweet chocolate chips
1/4   cup sugar
1/8   teaspoon salt
1/2   cup boiling water
1   cup whipping cream
1   quart milk, heated

Melt the chocolate chips in a double boiler over hot water. Stir in the sugar, salt and water. Cook for 10 minutes, stirring constantly. Cool to room temperature. Beat the whipping cream in a mixer bowl until soft peaks form. Fold in the cooled chocolate mixture.

To serve, spoon 2 tablespoons of the chocolate mixture into each cup. Fill with the heated milk and stir to blend well.

Serves 8

ALWAYS IN SEASON
The Junior League of Salt Lake City

MomMac's Boiled Custard

¹/₂   gallon milk
5   eggs
1¹/₃ cups sugar
¹/₄   cup all-purpose flour
1   teaspoon vanilla extract

Heat the milk in a saucepan over low to medium heat until steaming but not boiling. Combine the eggs, sugar, flour and vanilla in a bowl and mix well. Stir into the hot milk. Cook over low to medium heat until the mixture is thickened and coats the back of a spoon, stirring constantly. Remove from the heat and stir constantly until cool.

Serves a variable amount

RALPH AND DONNA McDONALD

*I awoke on Christmas morning 1941 to see Mother standing at the bedroom door with a big smile. She said, "Hurry! Santa was here last night!" Quickly slipping from under the covers onto the cold floor, I headed for the brightly lit cedar tree in the living room, where colorful gifts were piled underneath. Stockings hanging from the mantle were filled with bananas, apples, oranges, and little boxes of raisins.*

My eyes fell on a red scooter and several packages that read "To Ralph from Santa." I tore into the gifts, and to my delight, Santa left art supplies – modeling clay, crayons, watercolors, pencils, brushes, and pads of paper to draw and paint on. It was the perfect gift, and I have been creating art ever since.

Gifts from the Kitchen

I love giving gifts of food. I especially love giving home-baked goodies to family, friends, and the special people who help make my life run smoother: Domingo, who cares for my yard; John, who delivers my water; Hank, who delivers my mail; and that special neighbor who brings in my trash cans when I get home late.

As each year passes, I discover there are more and more helpful people in my life. So each year my gift baking escalates. Once when my husband couldn't find the kitchen counter or the dining room tabletop, he looked at my baking list and added up all of the quantities I had listed. Then he asked me, "So how many dozen cookies, biscotti, and truffles do you think you made?" I had only considered how many plates of food I needed to fill, so I told him I had no idea. He then boldly said, "It's eighty-four dozen. How did you do all of that in ten days?"

A few years ago, I thought I would start cutting back on my baking, and I got a bit behind my normal schedule, delivering my gifts later than usual. Boy, was I surprised when I walked into one office and was greeted with, "We were just talking about you and our favorite cookies and hoping you were still treating us!" What a wonderful experience, finding out how the small things you do for others affect them. After hearing that, I realized that with all of the craziness in our days, people love some things in life that are constant. I still haven't cut back on my baking because I love knowing people look forward to my plates of delectable homemade treats as much as I love making and giving them, and I promise, I'll keep my tradition going.

KAREN WARD

Christmas Gumdrop Bread

3   eggs
1   cup baking mix
1/2   cup sugar
1 1/2 teaspoons vanilla extract
1   (10-ounce) jar maraschino
      cherries, drained
1   cup dried apricots, chopped
1   cup pitted dates, chopped
1   cup small gumdrops
1   cup chopped walnuts or other nuts

Preheat the oven to 300 degrees. Beat the
eggs in a large bowl. Add the baking mix,
sugar and vanilla and mix well. Stir in
the cherries, apricots, dates, gumdrops
and walnuts. Divide the batter among
5 greased miniature loaf pans. Bake for
1 hour and 20 minutes or until a wooden
pick inserted in the center comes out
clean. Cool in the pans for 5 minutes.
Remove to wire racks to cool completely.
Batter may also be used to make muffins.

Makes 5 miniature loaves

BLACK TIE & BOOTS
University of Wyoming

Pecan Crescents

1   cup (2 sticks) butter, softened
      (do not substitute margarine)
1/4   cup confectioners' sugar
1/2   teaspoon salt
2   cups flour
1   tablespoon vanilla extract
2   cups chopped pecans
2   to 3 cups confectioners' sugar

Preheat the oven to 300 degrees. Cream
the butter, 1/4 cup confectioners' sugar
and salt in a mixing bowl until light and
fluffy. Add the flour and mix well. Mix
in the vanilla and pecans. Shape into
crescents and place on cookie sheets.
Bake for 10 to 12 minutes or just until
they begin to brown. Remove from the
cookie sheets and roll in additional
confectioners' sugar.

Makes 5 dozen

OH MY STARS!
The Junior League of Roanoke

Praline Cookies

1²/₃ cups flour
1¹/₂ teaspoons baking powder
¹/₂ teaspoon salt
¹/₂ cup (1 stick) butter or
   margarine, softened
1¹/₂ cups packed brown sugar
1 egg
1 teaspoon vanilla extract
1 cup pecan pieces
1¹/₂ cups whipping cream
1 cup packed brown sugar
1 cup confectioners' sugar

Preheat the oven to 350 degrees. Mix the flour, baking powder and salt in a bowl. Beat the butter in a mixer bowl until creamy. Add 1¹/₂ cups brown sugar. Beat until blended. Add the egg and vanilla and mix well. Add the dry ingredients gradually, beating well after each addition. Drop by rounded tablespoonfuls onto an ungreased cookie sheet. Bake for 10 minutes. Place 4 to 5 pecan pieces on top of each cookie. Cool on a wire rack for 5 to 10 minutes. Combine the cream and 1 cup brown sugar in a saucepan. Bring to a boil, stirring constantly. Boil for 2 minutes, stirring constantly. Remove from the heat. Add the confectioners' sugar and beat until smooth. Drizzle over the cookies.

Makes 2 dozen cookies

SOUTHERN ON OCCASION
The Junior League of Cobb-Marietta

Swedish Ginger Cookies

1 cup (2 sticks) butter, softened
1¹/₂ cups sugar
1 tablespoon light corn syrup
1 tablespoon molasses
2 teaspoons baking soda
1 egg
3³/₄ cups all-purpose flour
2 teaspoons cinnamon
1 teaspoon ginger
1 teaspoon ground cloves
¹/₄ teaspoon nutmeg
   Grated zest of 1 orange
2 tablespoons orange juice

Cream the butter and sugar in a mixing bowl until light and fluffy. Add the corn syrup, molasses, baking soda and egg and mix well. Sift the flour, cinnamon, ginger, cloves and nutmeg together and add to the creamed mixture. Stir in the orange zest and orange juice. Shape the dough into a ball. Chill until firm enough to roll. Preheat the oven to 350 degrees. Grease cookie sheets. Roll ¹/₈ inch thick on a floured surface. Cut into desired shapes and place on the prepared cookie sheets. Bake for 8 to 10 minutes. Cool on a wire rack. Store in an airtight container.

Makes about 70 cookies

TASTES, TALES AND TRADITIONS
Palo Alto Auxiliary

Heavenly Cranberry Bars

BARS
1 1/2 cups packed light brown sugar
1 cup (2 sticks) unsalted butter, melted and cooled
2 eggs
2 teaspoons vanilla extract
2 1/4 cups all-purpose flour
1 teaspoon baking powder
1 teaspoon salt
1 3/4 cups white chocolate chips
1 1/2 cups dried cranberries, coarsely chopped
1 cup toasted chopped pecans
1/4 cup grated orange zest

FROSTING
8 ounces cream cheese, at room temperature
1 cup confectioners' sugar
1/2 cup (1 stick) unsalted butter, at room temperature
3 tablespoons grated orange zest, divided
2 teaspoons vanilla extract
1/3 cup dried cranberries, coarsely chopped
6 ounces high quality white chocolate, coarsely chopped

For the bars, preheat the oven to 350 degrees. Lightly butter an 11×15-inch jelly roll pan or rimmed baking sheet. Whisk together the brown sugar, butter, eggs and vanilla in a large bowl until smooth. Whisk in the flour, baking powder and salt until well blended. Stir in the white chocolate chips, cranberries, pecans and orange zest. Spread the mixture evenly in the prepared pan (it will be quite stiff). Bake until golden brown, about 20 to 22 minutes. Set aside on a wire rack to cool.

For the frosting, cream together the cream cheese, confectioners' sugar, butter, 1 tablespoon orange zest and the vanilla with an electric mixer at medium speed until smooth and fluffy. Spread the mixture over the cooled bars. Stir together the remaining 2 tablespoons orange zest and dried cranberries in a small bowl. Sprinkle over the frosting. Melt the white chocolate in a small heatproof bowl set over a pan of simmering water, stirring until smooth. Drizzle the white chocolate over the bars and let sit until the chocolate is set. Cut the bars into 3-inch squares. Cut each square diagonally into triangles.

Makes 48 bars

CELEBRATE THE RAIN
The Junior League of Seattle

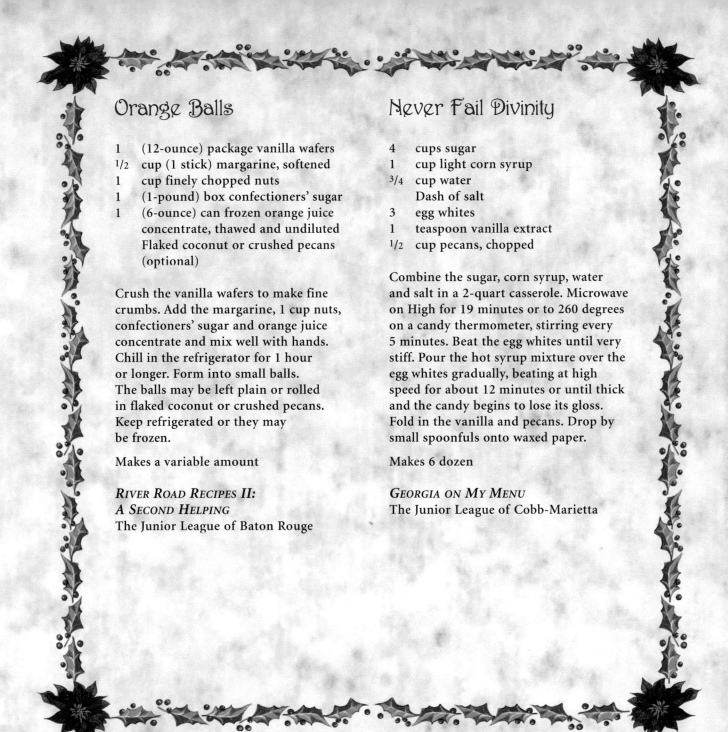

Orange Balls

1   (12-ounce) package vanilla wafers
1/2 cup (1 stick) margarine, softened
1   cup finely chopped nuts
1   (1-pound) box confectioners' sugar
1   (6-ounce) can frozen orange juice
     concentrate, thawed and undiluted
     Flaked coconut or crushed pecans
     (optional)

Crush the vanilla wafers to make fine crumbs. Add the margarine, 1 cup nuts, confectioners' sugar and orange juice concentrate and mix well with hands. Chill in the refrigerator for 1 hour or longer. Form into small balls. The balls may be left plain or rolled in flaked coconut or crushed pecans. Keep refrigerated or they may be frozen.

Makes a variable amount

RIVER ROAD RECIPES II:
A SECOND HELPING
The Junior League of Baton Rouge

Never Fail Divinity

4   cups sugar
1   cup light corn syrup
3/4 cup water
     Dash of salt
3   egg whites
1   teaspoon vanilla extract
1/2 cup pecans, chopped

Combine the sugar, corn syrup, water and salt in a 2-quart casserole. Microwave on High for 19 minutes or to 260 degrees on a candy thermometer, stirring every 5 minutes. Beat the egg whites until very stiff. Pour the hot syrup mixture over the egg whites gradually, beating at high speed for about 12 minutes or until thick and the candy begins to lose its gloss. Fold in the vanilla and pecans. Drop by small spoonfuls onto waxed paper.

Makes 6 dozen

GEORGIA ON MY MENU
The Junior League of Cobb-Marietta

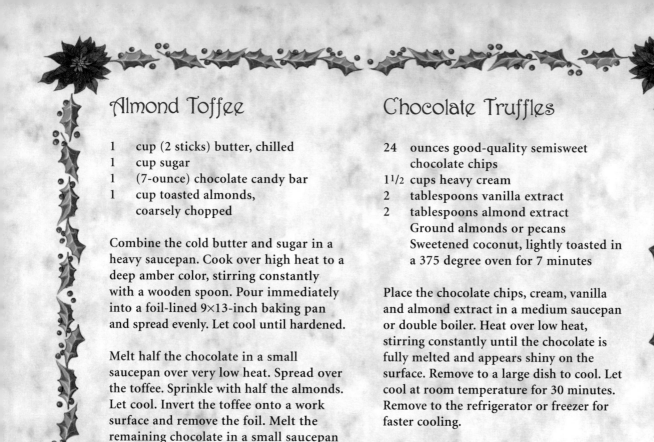

Almond Toffee

1 cup (2 sticks) butter, chilled
1 cup sugar
1 (7-ounce) chocolate candy bar
1 cup toasted almonds,
   coarsely chopped

Combine the cold butter and sugar in a heavy saucepan. Cook over high heat to a deep amber color, stirring constantly with a wooden spoon. Pour immediately into a foil-lined 9×13-inch baking pan and spread evenly. Let cool until hardened.

Melt half the chocolate in a small saucepan over very low heat. Spread over the toffee. Sprinkle with half the almonds. Let cool. Invert the toffee onto a work surface and remove the foil. Melt the remaining chocolate in a small saucepan over very low heat. Spread over the uncoated side of the toffee. Sprinkle with the remaining almonds. Break into pieces when cool.

Serves 24

PAR 3 TEA TIME AT THE MASTERS®
The Junior League of Augusta

Chocolate Truffles

24 ounces good-quality semisweet
    chocolate chips
1 1/2 cups heavy cream
2 tablespoons vanilla extract
2 tablespoons almond extract
   Ground almonds or pecans
   Sweetened coconut, lightly toasted in
   a 375 degree oven for 7 minutes

Place the chocolate chips, cream, vanilla and almond extract in a medium saucepan or double boiler. Heat over low heat, stirring constantly until the chocolate is fully melted and appears shiny on the surface. Remove to a large dish to cool. Let cool at room temperature for 30 minutes. Remove to the refrigerator or freezer for faster cooling.

In 1 hour, or when the chocolate is pliable yet firm (able to be scooped out with a spoon but maintain its shape), scoop out by small spoonfuls. Shape each scoopful into a ball and roll in the nuts or coconut. Store in the refrigerator until the chocoholic in you can't stand it and then serve.

Makes 50 truffles

STEAMBOAT SEASONS
Guild of Strings in the Mountains
Music Festival

White Chocolate Drops

16 ounces white chocolate, chopped
1/2 cup creamy peanut butter
1 1/2 cups crisp rice cereal
1 1/2 cups miniature marshmallows
1 cup unsalted dry-roasted peanuts
1/2 cup chocolate chips

Combine the white chocolate and peanut butter in a large heavy saucepan over low heat. Cook, stirring constantly, for 5 to 6 minutes or until smooth. Remove from the heat and stir in the rice cereal, marshmallows and peanuts. Drop by rounded spoonfuls onto a plastic wrap- or waxed paper-lined baking sheet. Chill for 10 minutes or until set.

Place the chocolate chips in a small heavy plastic sealable bag. Submerge the sealed bag in hot water until the chocolate is melted. Cut a tiny hole in one corner of the bag and drizzle the chocolate over the candies. Chill for 10 minutes. Store the candies in an airtight container.

Makes about 2 dozen candies

FROM THE COAST TO THE CASCADES
The Junior League of Eugene

Easy Caramel Corn

3 bags salted unbuttered microwave popcorn, popped
1 cup (2 sticks) butter
2 cups packed brown sugar
1/2 cup light corn syrup
1/2 teaspoon baking soda

Remove the unpopped kernels from the popped corn and place the popped corn in a large brown paper bag. Combine the butter, brown sugar and corn syrup in a medium saucepan over medium-high heat. Bring to a boil and boil for 5 minutes, stirring constantly. Remove from the heat and stir in the baking soda. Pour the caramel over the popped corn. Close the bag and shake well. Microwave on High for 2 minutes. Remove the bag and shake well. Spread over waxed paper to cool. The caramel will be very hot, so be careful.

Serves 12 to 16

GRAND TEMPTATIONS
The Junior League of Grand Rapids

Five-Pound Fudge

1	(12-ounce) can evaporated milk
4$^{1}/_{2}$	cups sugar
1$^{1}/_{2}$	cups (3 sticks) butter
11	ounces chocolate
24	ounces (4 cups) semisweet chocolate chips
2	cups (or more) marshmallow creme
1	teaspoon vanilla extract
1	cup chopped English walnuts

Combine the evaporated milk, sugar and butter in a heavy saucepan and bring to a boil. Cook for 5 minutes, stirring constantly. Remove from the heat and stir in the broken chocolate and chocolate chips until melted. Add the marshmallow creme and beat until smooth. Stir in the vanilla and walnuts. Pour into 2 greased 9×13-inch dishes. Let stand until cool. Chill in the refrigerator for 1 to 2 hours or until firm. Cut into squares. Store in the refrigerator or freezer.

Makes 10 dozen

FIRST IMPRESSIONS
The Junior League of
Waterloo-Cedar Falls

Incredible Fudge

12	ounces Velveeta cheese
1	cup (2 sticks) butter or margarine
6	(1-ounce) squares unsweetened baking chocolate
2	tablespoons Country Bob's All Purpose Original Sauce
2	(1-pound) packages confectioners' sugar
1	teaspoon vanilla extract
1$^{1}/_{2}$	cups chopped pecans (optional)

Place the Velveeta, butter, chocolate and Country Bob's All Purpose Original Sauce in a large microwave-safe bowl. Microwave on High for 2 to 4 minutes, stirring every minute until the mixture is smooth and well blended. Place the confectioners' sugar in a large mixing bowl. Add the chocolate mixture gradually, beating with an electric mixer at medium speed until well blended after each addition. Beat in the vanilla. Stir in the pecans. Pour the fudge into a greased 9×13-inch pan. Smooth the top. Cover and refrigerate for several hours or until firm. Cut into squares. Store in the refrigerator.

Makes 4 pounds

*THE ORIGINAL COUNTRY BOB'S
COOKBOOK*
Country Bob, Inc.

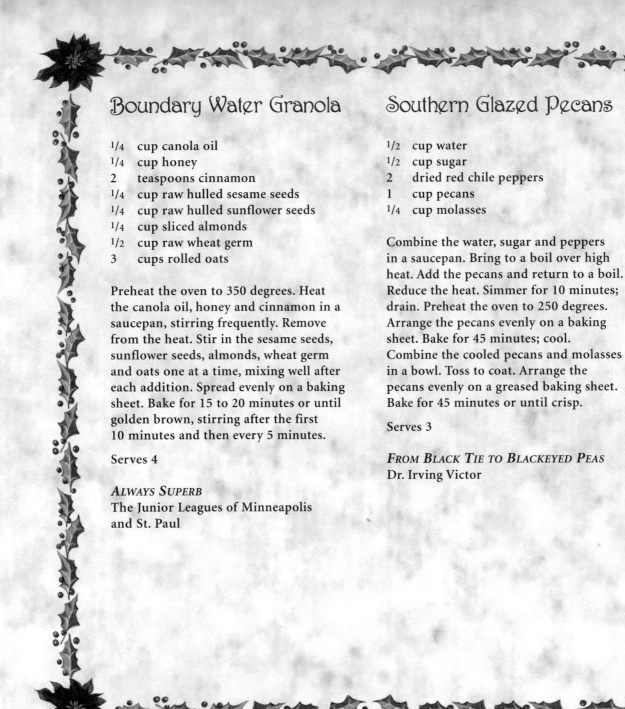

Boundary Water Granola

1/4   cup canola oil
1/4   cup honey
2   teaspoons cinnamon
1/4   cup raw hulled sesame seeds
1/4   cup raw hulled sunflower seeds
1/4   cup sliced almonds
1/2   cup raw wheat germ
3   cups rolled oats

Preheat the oven to 350 degrees. Heat the canola oil, honey and cinnamon in a saucepan, stirring frequently. Remove from the heat. Stir in the sesame seeds, sunflower seeds, almonds, wheat germ and oats one at a time, mixing well after each addition. Spread evenly on a baking sheet. Bake for 15 to 20 minutes or until golden brown, stirring after the first 10 minutes and then every 5 minutes.

Serves 4

ALWAYS SUPERB
The Junior Leagues of Minneapolis and St. Paul

Southern Glazed Pecans

1/2   cup water
1/2   cup sugar
2   dried red chile peppers
1   cup pecans
1/4   cup molasses

Combine the water, sugar and peppers in a saucepan. Bring to a boil over high heat. Add the pecans and return to a boil. Reduce the heat. Simmer for 10 minutes; drain. Preheat the oven to 250 degrees. Arrange the pecans evenly on a baking sheet. Bake for 45 minutes; cool. Combine the cooled pecans and molasses in a bowl. Toss to coat. Arrange the pecans evenly on a greased baking sheet. Bake for 45 minutes or until crisp.

Serves 3

FROM BLACK TIE TO BLACKEYED PEAS
Dr. Irving Victor

Curried Pumpkin Seeds

1²/₃ cups warm water
¹/₃ cup curry powder
Juice of 1 lime
1 teaspoon salt
1 garlic clove, finely minced
2¹/₃ cups hulled pumpkin seeds
Butter to taste
Salt to taste

Combine ²/₃ cup of the warm water and the curry powder in a saucepan and mix well. Add the lime juice, 1 teaspoon salt and the garlic, stirring until blended. Stir in the remaining cup warm water. Cook until heated through, stirring constantly. Add the pumpkin seeds and mix well. Simmer for 5 minutes, stirring frequently; do not boil. Preheat the oven to 250 degrees. Drain and spread the pumpkin seeds in a single layer on a baking sheet. Dot with butter; sprinkle with salt. Bake until crisp. Let stand until cool. Store in an airtight container.

Makes 2¹/₃ cups

TEXAS TIES
The Junior League of North Harris and South Montgomery Counties

Tangy Toasted Nuts

2 tablespoons Worcestershire sauce
2 tablespoons melted butter
2 tablespoons Parmesan cheese (fresh if available)
¹/₂ teaspoon red pepper
1¹/₂ cups walnuts, pecans or clean and dry pumpkin seeds

Preheat the oven to 350 degrees. Combine the Worcestershire sauce, butter, Parmesan cheese and red pepper in a bowl and mix well. Add the nuts and toss to coat well. Spread evenly on a baking sheet. Toast for 15 minutes for the walnuts or pecans or for 30 minutes for the pumpkin seeds. Store in an airtight container.

Serves 6 to 8

OF TIDE & THYME
The Junior League of Annapolis

Cranberry Chutney

1/2 cup peeled and chopped apple
1 to 2 tablespoons lemon juice
2 cups fresh cranberries
1/2 cup water
1/2 cup raisins
1 small onion, chopped
1 scant cup sugar
1/4 teaspoon ginger
1/4 teaspoon cinnamon
1/8 teaspoon ground allspice
1/8 teaspoon salt
1 (8-ounce) can crushed pineapple (in its own juice)
1/4 cup chopped celery
1/4 cup chopped pecans or walnuts

Sprinkle the apples with the lemon juice. Combine the cranberries, water, raisins, onion, sugar, ginger, cinnamon, allspice and salt in a Dutch oven. Cook, uncovered, over medium heat for 15 minutes or until the cranberry skins pop. Stir in the pineapple and juice, celery, pecans and apples. Reduce the heat to low. Cook, uncovered, for 30 minutes, stirring frequently. Serve warm or chilled.

Makes 3 1/2 cups

SECOND ROUND, TEA-TIME AT THE MASTERS®
The Junior League of Augusta

Polk Pickles

1/2 package pickling spices
1 gallon sour jumbo pickles, drained
4 1/2 pounds sugar
2 heads garlic, separated into cloves

Wrap the pickling spices in cheesecloth and secure with kitchen twine. Cut the tips from the ends of the pickles and discard. Cut each pickle into 1/4- to 1/2-inch slices. Alternate layers of the sliced pickles, sugar and garlic cloves in a 2-gallon crock until all of the ingredients are used. Add the cheesecloth bag. Let stand, covered, at room temperature for 5 days, stirring each morning. Transfer the pickle mixture to a gallon jar, discarding the spices and garlic. Store, covered, in the refrigerator.

PROVISIONS & POLITICS
James K. Polk Memorial Association

Hot Chocolate Mix

1   (25-ounce) box nonfat dry
    milk powder
1   (1-pound) can chocolate drink mix
1   (1-pound) package
    confectioners' sugar
1   (1-pound) jar nondairy
    coffee creamer

Combine the milk powder, drink mix,
confectioners' sugar and coffee creamer
in a bowl. Store in an airtight container
at room temperature. For each cup of hot
chocolate, combine $1/2$ cup hot water with
$1/2$ cup hot chocolate mix; mix well.

Makes 50 servings

ONCE UPON A TIME
The Junior League of Evansville

*Package the mix in airtight holiday
containers. Attach a scoop, peppermint
sticks and recipe card with raffia.*

Cinnamon Ornaments

1   cup plus 2 tablespoons cinnamon
1   tablespoon ground cloves
1   tablespoon nutmeg
$3/4$ cup applesauce
2   tablespoons white glue

Combine the cinnamon, cloves and
nutmeg in a bowl and mix well. Stir in the
applesauce and glue. Mix the applesauce
mixture with your hands until smooth.
Divide the dough into 2 equal portions.
Roll each portion $1/4$ inch thick on a hard
surface and cut with the desired cookie
cutters. Make a hole in each ornament
with a drinking straw. Dry the ornaments
on wire racks for several days. Attach
the desired decorations with craft glue.
Thread ribbon through the holes and tie
the ends into bows.

Makes for fun

HOME AGAIN, HOME AGAIN
The Junior League of Owensboro

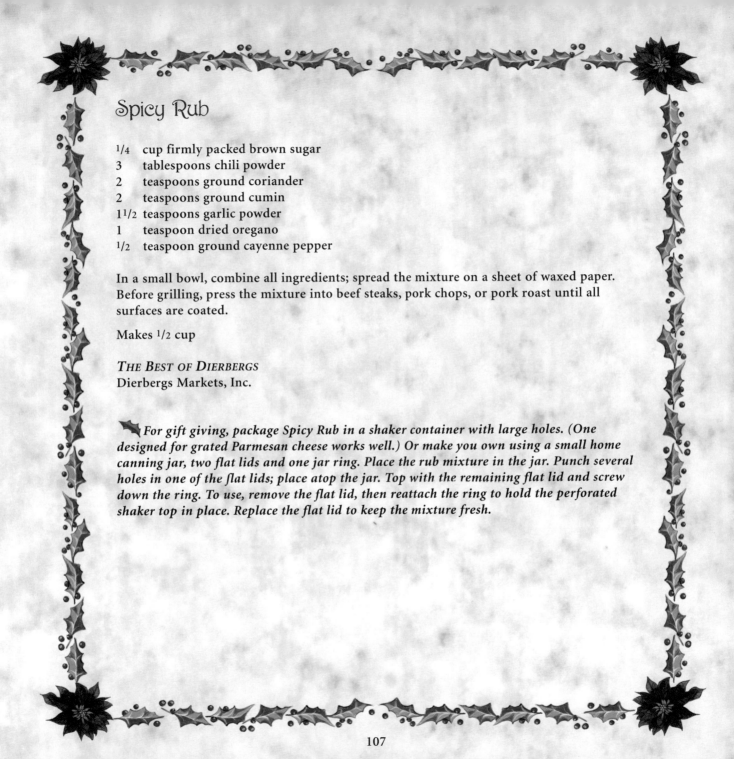

Spicy Rub

1/4   cup firmly packed brown sugar
3   tablespoons chili powder
2   teaspoons ground coriander
2   teaspoons ground cumin
1 1/2   teaspoons garlic powder
1   teaspoon dried oregano
1/2   teaspoon ground cayenne pepper

In a small bowl, combine all ingredients; spread the mixture on a sheet of waxed paper. Before grilling, press the mixture into beef steaks, pork chops, or pork roast until all surfaces are coated.

Makes 1/2 cup

THE BEST OF DIERBERGS
Dierbergs Markets, Inc.

For gift giving, package Spicy Rub in a shaker container with large holes. (One designed for grated Parmesan cheese works well.) Or make you own using a small home canning jar, two flat lids and one jar ring. Place the rub mixture in the jar. Punch several holes in one of the flat lids; place atop the jar. Top with the remaining flat lid and screw down the ring. To use, remove the flat lid, then reattach the ring to hold the perforated shaker top in place. Replace the flat lid to keep the mixture fresh.

Index

About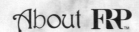

FRP (Favorite Recipes Press), located in Nashville, Tennessee, is one of the nation's best-known and respected cookbook companies. FRP began by publishing cookbooks for its parent company, Southwestern/Great American in 1961. Since then, FRP has grown to be an important and successful division of the company, producing hundreds of titles for nonprofit organizations, companies, and individuals.

FRP works with many different entities, each with its own unique structure and needs. The company's achievements are directly related to a strong commitment to the success of each customer served. Full support, consultation, and an array of professional services are available every step of the way in the creation, production, and marketing of your self-published cookbook.

In 2005, FRP started its own publishing division. FRP titles include:
Almost Homemade: Cake Mix Desserts $9.95
My Favorite Recipes: Capture Your Family's Favorite Recipes and Traditions $12.95
The Vintner's Table: Recipes From A Winery Chef $24.95

Cookbooks published by FRP and its clients are available for purchase through The Cookbook Marketplace. You will find an impressive assortment of cookbooks from across the country, many of which are award-winning titles.

Order information:
Order online at www.cookbookmarketplace.com
Order toll-free 1-800-269-6839

The Cookbook Marketplace
2451 Atrium Way
Nashville, TN 37214

If you are interested in publishing a new cookbook or reprinting an existing title, please contact us at www.frpbooks.com.